Social Media Aspects:

Social Media Activism

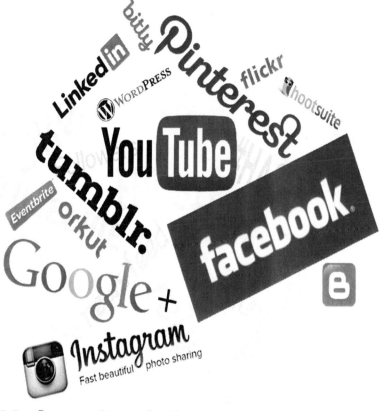

Using Social Media for Your Cause or Campaign

4th Edition
Dave Pratt Carter
Edited by Mary López-Carter

About the Author

Dave Carter is an experienced political candidate for public office. He took time off for to run for office from his 'normal job' of Social Media mentoring, coaching and application support/development. Although he develops custom Facebook, Twitter and web applications, his fondness is for teaching. He is involved with Mobile Web and Mobile App development for the small business of iDesign Media Solutions.

When he's not 'geeking out' (as the family describes it), he's involved with outdoor adventures (SCUBA, hiking, skiing, and more) and spends a lot of time with his three boys and wife, Mary.

He's written numerous articles for various publications on the topics of Client-Server technologies, Business Intelligence, Social Media and Mobile technologies.

He welcomes invitations for speaking events, dive trips and cooking classes.

Training and Consulting

iDesign offers training for Social Media, multimedia design and other emerging topics. Contact them at training@iDesignMobileApps.com or sales@iDesignMobileApps.com

Acknowledgements

I would like to thank those people who have helped me expand the reach I have with the skills I have learned.

- Mary López-Carter: Always a coach, teammate and cheerleader

- Dutch, Chris and Jon: Three good reasons to try harder with all things

Fourth Edition Notes

The first editions of this book were written with the intention of helping local (NC) groups. When it was reviewed outside of the local reach, the feedback led to more research and discussion of what needs to go into a second edition. This ended up needing changes because of the changes in technology. Suddenly, we have a third then a fourth edition.

Since the social media technology changes so rapidly, it is almost impossible (unless in electronic form) to produce a completely current set of standards and procedures to help everyone with social media. However, we decided that it was possible to give a really good shotgun approach, in a small (primer) form.

The third edition incorporated a rather significant update for content. This is mainly because of the wealth of changes on the platforms (such as Facebook) plus the continued growth of other platforms (Instagram for one).

Incorporated within this book, we have updated the information for new releases of software (and websites). This may have changed already, but the information is still sound. Since the electronic version (Kindle, on Amazon.com) is slightly easier to keep updated, there will be quarterly updates to the Kindle and only yearly (estimated) changes to the printed version.

Forward

In 'Social Media for Activism' Dave Pratt Carter is uniquely on target. Social Media has become your most viable link to the outside world; especially the one that you would like to influence as it relates to business, current news and politics.

I administer more web sites, Facebook pages, Twitter accounts and other social media applications than I care to mention. There are so many choices available now that weren't around in 2008, when I first became aware that social media could get your message in front of many more willing eyeballs, without constantly triggering email spam filters, etc.

If you apply the principles in Dave's book will save you a lot of time sorting the wheat from the chaff, helping you to hone your approach to maximize your influence and to keep you from making common mistakes that negatively affect your credibility and the audience you are trying to reach.

For example, If you want to be successful you need to understand that you use # (hashtags) in Twitter when you want to broadcast a message to as many interest groups as possible and the @ symbol when you want to narrowcast your message to specific targets.

'Social Media for Activism' is an easy read and well worth your time, no matter which audience you are aiming for.

-Bob Diamond RPh
Google.com/+BobDiamondRPh

Tell us what you Think

iDesign Media Solutions and Dave Carter believe in customized solutions and personal (and social) relationships. When writing materials such as this, creating web content and technology solutions, the team at iDesign strives to create a strong connection and deliver the best solutions to each customer.

If you have suggestions for improvement, future training, mobile apps, or just want to share a recipe or secret SCUBA location, get in touch with us:

David@iDesignMobileApps.com

info@iDesignMobileApps.com

Table of Contents

Introduction

I've been using social media tools for years. I admit that I've used MySpace, IRC, and other social tools in the past. I am excited over the prospect of what social media tools will give us in the months and years to come.

When I got involved with local politics and activism, I was already deeply into Social Media technologies. I assisted my wife with her startup company, iDesign Mobile Apps (now iDesign Media Solutions), by coding what her developers couldn't or didn't have time to complete. I am a team player, most days. Much of my work is done for free – because I believe in the missions of the various organizations who seek my help.

This involvement led me to helping others locally set up their social media presence. Not just individuals, but organizations, businesses and causes were asking for help. I realized that the 'simple' stuff of social media wasn't so simple for many people.

This book was created to help those involved in campaigns, causes and other forms of activism to create a winning social media plan and execute it. While I don't dig deeply into the nuances of branding, marketing plan execution and activist messaging, I do summarize for the average person a path to get their program moving.

There are already books that cover the bases on that in-depth Social Media pretty well. Instead, I wanted to help people get their campaign moving quickly – without them having to read volumes of social media theory and methodology. Basically, I wanted a quick start guide to Social Media for activists.

I presented this information to a group concerned with the environment and another concerned with over-taxation in NC. Both groups agreed that they sorely needed help with their social media programming but had no idea where or how to start.

This book will help people overcome the fear of social media and technology. This book can be used as a starter for nearly any campaign in social media – even outside of activism. The good thing about most social media tools: They are pretty easy to get proficiency once you get started. So, this booklet should give you the 'nudge' you need to get started.

As you read this material, understand that the notion of 'one size fits all' really only works for a small portion of the population. You should take the material from this guide and apply it as it makes sense to you and your cause. Also, I cover the big players in Social Media in the guide. I address Facebook, YouTube, Google+ and Twitter. I use and appreciate others like Pinterest and Tumblr and can see how these tools will help a cause. But, they aren't likely to be the main tools for any campaign. The main coverage concentrates on the biggest return to address the majority of cause-based activism. You should, however, feel free to investigate other social media tools for all campaigns.

What is Social Media?

Social Media is an often-used term that may mean different things to different people. For example, some may think of Facebook and Twitter as real social media tools and exclude YouTube and Blogs. Nonetheless, Social Media has multiple face or aspects that can be explored for use by organizations to further their causes, promote products and market services.

One social media site, Wikipedia (whether this is a Social Media site is really up to you and your definition – stay with me here), explains Social Media: *Refers to the means of interactions among people in which they create, share, and exchange information and ideas in virtual communities and networks*. While dictionary.com reveals Social Media is: Web sites and other online means of communication that are used by large groups of people to share information and to develop social and professional contacts.

Social media accounts for every 1 out of 6 minutes spent on line (for the average online user, based upon sampling).

If you use Facebook or Twitter or Pinterest to communicate to your social or professional contacts, then they are Social Media sites. Email is a form of social media, but we simply call it "email". Plus, it's not centered on a community quite like a social media tool may be. Other sites may be pulled into the Social Media envelope simply because they allow people to convey information to a broad audience through information sharing (such as Wikipedia or a blog).

For the sake of this book, we will stick with the general definition of social media that exists in Dictionary.com. Examples of various social media aspects

3

and sites will be provided to help round out your understanding.

Additionally, when you are able to engage others in content you create in a "social context" we will investigate its use as a social media. This means that YouTube is included (as well as Vine and Vimeo) since it leads to social engagement and dialogue.

What Makes Social Media Work for Activism?

Social media provides an outlet that can take multiple channels for distribution of a message. Additionally, it allows, in most cases, for the creation of a dialogue in a social setting (open to larger numbers of people). Compare this to email. In email, you have to already know the email address of the target audience(s) for the message. You can hope to send the message to people and have it distributed by them (forwarding), but this happening is unlikely.

As activism goes, you want to reach as many 'listeners' (whether it's readers or actual listeners) to your message as possible. Paid advertising is somewhat effective, but spreading an activist message via a billboard or radio ad is not only costly, but it is often not able to hit the key demographics for your particular message. This is because the common billboard is more likely to communicate with anyone who happens by compared to a more targeted audience. For the price, a billboard or similar "Paid" media is far too expensive to utilize for a campaign.

It is important to note that social media does not replace traditional forms of advocacy or organizing. It is a tool to augment this and the messaging associated.

Gathering thousands of Likes in Facebook and hundreds of Followers in Twitter does not directly compare to votes for or against a stance. The likes and follows in social media help you partially gauge your reach (for the messaging). **Never** consider the total number of Likes or Follows (Facebook and Twitter respectively) to be the true extent of your reach. In fact, many people will see and be affected by your messaging who will not Like or Follow you.

Social media can be used to expand the awareness in the communities affected. It's far more common to have people discuss a YouTube video or clever Facebook meme than a billboard they passed while driving to the store or office. If you're already in Facebook, then you know that you may have already shared a meme or image that impressed you. When was the last time you discussed a billboard ad while standing at the water cooler or coffee station at the office?

In order to grow, you need to expand your presence: Not only in the physical world, but also in the social *mediasphere*. Growing requires content and messaging, sharing and integration, content publishing (web sites and beyond) and analysis of what works and what doesn't.

Keys to Your Success

Social media allows for you to share information with others without having to push the information to individuals. You may recall the old Ron Popeil expression, "Set it and forget it!" You can appreciate that a lot of social media work will continue beyond a post being placed. A well-executed campaign will keep sharing with others beyond the initial post.

SHARE AND MEASURE

How do you gauge success with social media? How can you tell if you have changed the sentiment regarding your cause? Is the sentiment improved? Do you have advocates joining the cause? How broadly did you reach with your messaging?

You will need to establish a plan with your social media program to ensure that you know the answers to questions like this. If you don't know them, you will need a way to discover them. Executing a broad-base social media plan without direction is likely to waste time and energy and may likely confuse your messaging.

When all is said and done, you need to be able to review your plan and see whether the improvements expected were made. From time to time, do a reality check on the overall social media plan and determine where improvements must be made. While the messages can be "set it and forget it" (letting your network do it's job), the messaging process is not.

Taking a Stand on Issues

When you are actively commenting or you are the creator of a post (on an issue) in social media, you're in the minority. A study has revealed that majority of people are only spectators, lurkers, viewers and consumers of online posts while the very small minority are the authors or commentators. Getting involved gives you the chance to take a stand and be seen. This doesn't mean take a stand on EVERY issue, but take stands on issues where you have strength and a defensible position.

When you create a post that marks your position on an issue, people will have opportunity to read your stance then they will make a decision. Some will actually comment and become part of the minority. Whether they differ in opinion from you or not, their involvement brings others into the mix. When you own the issue and your position on it, you (acting as the creator or the commentator) will be able to influence people to take action (if action is needed). People will decide whether you are correct or incorrect. People will decide whether they will pursue the issue by researching, commenting or forwarding (sharing) with others. Taking a stand on an issue also gives people a way to identify with you. People who share your viewpoints on issues will often 'side' with you on other issues that may not have a strong opinion.

Making a Brand stand OUT!

Whether you're a fan of "Story Branding" or one of the classic (range, corporate, or unique) branding strategies, you're going to have to have a clear idea of your branding approach before you implement a social media program for your cause. Since the coverage of this book is not designed to be a primer on marketing and branding strategies, it's worthwhile to mention that it is a good idea to research what branding tools have been successful with your particular cause. Re-purposing older tools is often the simplest and most successful method used.

Your cause will need an image. Logos work in your branding. Couple this with your messaging (consistent, clear...) and you have the basis for your social media campaigns.

If you think about it, your cause can easily get lost in a sea of other issues, causes, cases and activism. Additionally, there's also a wealth of other competitors for your audience's attention. You must be able to have your particular branding STAND OUT against the myriad choices.

A friend once told me, "The Secret to Branding is the three Ns: Name, Niche and 'Nique."I ignored that he cheated with the third N for Unique. Nonetheless, your social media branding needs to have the name that will POP for the readers and viewers. It must fit into the niche for the marketplace. And the message coupled with the brand must be unique (this is what makes it stand out).

With your naming, you can find resources online and in printed texts covering the best way to come up with a name. Your organization's name can be used with your social media campaign branding or it can be a separate name altogether. Either way, this name must help convey to the audience the attributes necessary to create an understanding of the brand.

Niche is easily overlooked when it comes to activism. Organizations create their campaigns and charge forward without thinking about how they fit into the whole scheme of things. What specific needs are being addressed by the organization for the community and target audience? What can characterize the cause? How are competitive causes and groups positioning themselves? It is vital to be clear with the niche as you devise your branding, as you will be able to create direct relations to your campaign in social media from the niche components.

Uniqueness helps set your branding apart from the crowd. It's OK to say your organization is for "protection of animal rights". But, can you tell what organization this is with this one statement? Not really. Create a very simple statement or series of statements that work tightly with your branding to help create the special and unique position of your cause. You should strive to set yourself apart from competition with a clear contrast.

Connecting to Create Community

The media offerings have changed dramatically in the last decade. Gone are the days when you read stuff on newspaper and magazine, watch news or documentary on television. We get news faster via Twitter and Facebook than we do via traditional means. People like you and me are using gadgets (iPhones, iPads, Android Phones...) to be the reporters in the field without being journalists. People can connect far easier than they did a mere decade ago.

You have to consider social networking communities as groups of migrant audiences. This is why a successful campaign has multiple spokes to bring people into a single or grouped hub. Take, for instance, the once very popular MySpace. It was the big deal in social media at one time. Now, it's no longer highly regarded, but it does have a presence still. Social media sites can be used for a while then may fall in their popularity. If you've invested a great deal of time in only one site, your community may fall away as well.

Even though it is a bit older, Social media has had 8 years of stellar growth in the business, academic, media and other industries. The use of social media by groups for social good has been steadily on the rise.

Keep in mind that with your cause, you need to create connections to people. Marketing is not the primary goal of your social media campaign; it's a component of the campaign. The primary goal of any good social media campaign is to create a broader network of connections. Creating Connections for Community and Cause. Just consider it as CCCC.

You want to connect with people. Connections can create followers of your brand (your cause). It is possible to build thousands of relationships through social media campaigns. Each connection can lead to a more mature relationship that can benefit and propel your mission.

One of the principal benefits to leveraging social media for your campaigns is globalization. This gives you access to people outside of your geographic communities. This gives you reach far beyond what you'd expect from any campaign with traditional campaigns (even with direct mail, your scope is limited and each interaction is typically 1:1).

By simply beginning a campaign with a key cadre of social media workers and using them to build a small and passionate network of people who care about the cause, you can quickly build viral mass. Remember, you want to make relationships with people. Social media will give you opportunities as your contacts/connections grow. You can make real relationships. Those relationships can bring donations, more activists, and ideas to the cause.

Be Engaging

Social Media can be useful to attract new people to your cause. It allows you to drop off information (on a site) and have literally thousands of people exposed to it. That information should have something to attract their attention. If you're already experienced in Facebook, then you know what turns you on from other people's posts. It may be a post about a recipe, a toy poodle, or a butterfly. For activism, it may be about a political position, a controversial statement made by a candidate for public office, or just a well stated challenge you create and post. Making people think is a good mission for each of your posts in social media. If you want to have people read these posts, being engaging is key.

When you have dialogue that is created from an engaging conversation (triggered by a good topic, perhaps), you will automatically gain more views and perhaps more involved in the dialogue. This engagement is vital to the success of your social media communication and campaign success.

Don't be afraid to 'jump in' and get your feet wet. In fact, the more you are able to express what you are pondering, the more engaging you become. When you challenge the status quo, when you shock people and when you make them think, you are far more likely to get more people actively engaged in your posts.

If you are a perceptive person, then you may already know what makes your audience "tick". Knowing what opinions are they likely to have and what motivates them will help you create the best statements to challenge them and to give them the urge to engage in dialogue with you. This gives you an "in" to challenge their positions. This gives you the engagement when they reply and perhaps defend their position. A defense gives you more information on them. The more information on the conversation's parties means more challenges or stimulation.

You may realize that this may lead to some animosity or perhaps, worse, some anger. When engaging others you may step on toes, after all, the toes are virtual. This will likely make more people pay attention to you – for better or worse. Just take a look at the followers in Twitter (or Facebook) for Rush Limbaugh or Al Sharpton!

You Pick your Battles

When I discussed engaging conversation, I mentioned that you should challenge people. Challenges give you an avenue to introduce new ideas and information that may influence others – even if those people are on the sidelines.

There is remarkable potential for success – and failure – for a project with social media. If done well, social networks can be built and provide for rapid message spreading, common goal creation and expanded connections established. The right message component at the right time in the right way (think about the way Viral messages or videos in YouTube spread) can be spectacularly powerful.

You have to keep an eye opened to the technologies being used. The Web and the tools housed within are in flux constantly. The web and the tools used with it are constantly being changed. New technologies, new tools, new ways to employ them and more are being devised daily.

There is no one-size-fits-all solution with your campaign. Email, while dwindling in popularity, is still highly effective for communications.

Build Expertise

As you spread your message, your credibility will build as you continue with your stances. Having consistency in your messaging and your ideals is key to this. If you seem wishy-washy, people will turn on you. If you are steadfast and keep your message clean, you will have people against you and people for you, but your proponents will likely stay as proponents and not turn neutral or against you.

As you stick to your messaging, make sure you keep educating yourself and passing along what you learn to others – both in your network and via social media. This will help others to learn from you and regard you as the expert and worthy of a follow or a read or the attention to the messages in general. This is vital. Imagine hearing a message from a person who never rides the bus talking about the best way to catch a bus to a particular location. Their information may be credible, but not on face value. They've no established expertise and personal credibility on the topic. If the same person had a message on diets and they happen to be a dietician, then you're more likely to be aware and respectful of the message.

Expert status is not difficult to attain. Sometimes, readers are simply satisfied with a title associated with your name (PhD, for example). Other times, a list of your works (like an author) or publications in your profile is effective. But, it's also possible to build simply by having your name associated with the topic or cause long enough to build 'legs' or staying power. There are many activists on the left and right who aren't really experts in their fields. They are simply associated with the causes and well respected even though their technical basis on what they espouse may be weak or non-existent. I don't suggest you follow this path. It's always good to learn as much as you can as often as you can to stay on top of the issues, the technical details and the policies associated with your cause. Do not let others define you and your cause. Be the expert and define it yourself.

There's also the possibility that you are acting on behalf of a cause where you can't always establish yourself as the expert. This shouldn't stop you from working to establish the "account" as a source of honest information and opinion. This will make you as a source more credible. This may take longer, considering the anonymity, but it can work. Consider the trustworthiness of an organization such as LifeLock when they speak on Identity Theft and protection as an example.

Getting The Masses Home

Successful social media programs always have a way to give people more information. The destination for most of your messaging is the people who will connect with you in some way. You need to transform them into activists or donors in some way. This means you need to convert them from interested parties to participants. The conversion and transformation processes are typically not something that you can execute on the Social Media tool set.

Websites provide a doorway into the cause's key collateral. Twitter limits your words (140 characters). Facebook is only useful if the audience is using Facebook. Websites are more universal. The website must provide the message receiver with the most compelling reasons to join the cause.

Social media is a tool that will help you (when used properly) bring people from a general interest point of view. Simply said, your social media program needs to attract people to get more information. This information is housed at your website (home).

A well designed home page and site for your cause can make a difference in conversion.

In addition to bringing people "home" to find a wealth of additional information, your website should be filled with useful tools, tips, memes, graphics, infographics and other items that can be readily shared on the visitors' own social media accounts. This is done using commercially available tools from organizations such as ShareThis and AddThis. With either of these toolsets, you can create a more engaging web site that makes sharing with the outside world a simple click and share process.

Capitalize on your Network

Social media is important for branding and generating buzz. Lead generation is a natural offshoot from this. The leads generated from social media can lead to the activism participants that you need. Building leads begins with every 'friendly' lead you already have: All those associated in existing members' networks.

Each member of the social media team should work with the other members of the cause. Existing social networks should be tapped (wherever applicable) to springboard the effort of your channels. Not using existing networks is a common mistake with many cause-based marketing efforts.

Use your team's social channels to provide both subtle and overt relationships to the cause branding. Getting the friends of friends involved is often easier than getting those unfamiliar involved. You should recall that the whole effort of social media channels often hinges upon "peer recommendation". If you recommend a cause to your friends, they are more likely to join in with you than they would if they received an unsolicited request from another unknown party.

Take advantage of each email address, social media friend and physical address (for mailings) of all existing networks you have. Tap into this network first – as you push your channels.

Building your Social Media Team

The scope of your social media projects will help you determine the size of the team you will need. However, from a practical standpoint, you may not have the time needed to fully implement all aspects of your social media plan. If you're like many who "give it a go" in social media programs, you wear all the hats and try to do everything. This may actually succeed in some situations – despite your own efforts. A reasonable structure can be built with a platform expert for each social media channel reporting to an overall program manager. The titles you use don't matter, but the functions of each do. In this simple structure, the channel experts are going to be individuals who have skills on the particular channels (such as Facebook and Twitter). The program manager will be the person who makes sure the various channels are using the messaging properly (from the marketing perspective). They will likely not need to get into any of the technical aspects of the various channels.

If you had a larger group to build a stronger structure, you will be able to direct resources more fully to the channels which need more exposure and that will carry more of the messaging. Consider this: Pinterest may be a good social media channel for your group. However, it may only need to have fewer posts (Pins) than the comparative channel for Facebook or Twitter. One person may be able to manage the Pinterest channel (and maybe others) while three people manage the Facebook channel alone.

How you build your team will also depend upon other skills (interpersonal, professional, functional) that need to be considered for project success. Starting out, the program manager needs to ensure that the teams have achievable goals, clearly defined missions, understandable messages and access to the social media tools. Build a schedule and assign tasks for each member of the team. Develop a follow-up plan for the channels and for the team as a whole – especially since the messaging should be consistent.

Be Clear with all "Calls to Action"

You have your campaign messaging created. You know who your audience is. You know which platforms you are going to target and which channels will be used. And now you start posting your content everywhere. Right?

Well, not exactly.

Your messaging is likely to lead people to a call to action. The call to action may sound foreign, but you're likely familiar with it. Think about the commercials on TV that end with "call now, while supplies last" or similar. Each of these expressions is a *call to action*.

When you employ social media messages to further the effectiveness of your cause, you will need to be clear with your calls to action. Make sure that the messages that support recruiting or outreach include the call to action needed to 'tie things together'.

The example below may seem simple, but it's effective. The call bubble points to a button for "Like" on Facebook. This call to action graphic can be used on a web site or within another graphic (carefully placed to point to the Like button). Similar graphics or text can be used within other social media channels.

Click Here to Like Us on

Register Right Now!

The Basics 1: Call to Action Graphics

Scoring Engagement of your SM Team

As you work through your campaigns, you will evaluate how to engage your target audience on a more personal level, relay to them the value of taking action (joining the cause, donating, etc.), and ultimately move them to becoming involved in some way.

If you set goals such as "Reach *n* Twitter followers" then you have a goal that may be achievable, but not valuable. When you've set your goals for Twitter followers to engage (with a call to action) on the home page (your targeted web site) to Sign up, to Donate, or similar, then you have measurable and useful goals. Similarly, attaining a certain number of Facebook Likes on a page or a post may not be as valuable as actionable points for website visits from a specific post.

I've always suggested that a new campaign have three to five clearly defined goals. If you set *"increase hits to xyz page on website by 150%"* and have a good baseline of your current hits on that page, this would qualify as a reasonable goal.

Since there are many ways to engage your activists, you will need to find quantifiable ways to evaluate what is successful.

Let's consider an email campaign as a portion of your social media outreach. A newsletter is created using a tool such as Constant Contact. Each "Open" (in the reports of Constant Contact) for every target e-mail is scored. Each click on a link embedded within the email is also scored. You can evaluate where the more engaged email addressees are simply by scanning the total points earned by the various email addresses.

You need to decide what length of time is needed to reach that goal or to test for that objective. For example, if you have the prior 150% growth on a specific page and allow for three years to attain it, this isn't a reasonable goal. If you want to hit that goal within 30 days, it's likely you will have a more effective campaign metric. Remember, your online presence with Social Media should be an ongoing enterprise. However, each action you take with the platforms should be with a clear mission, goals, and metrics associated.

What do you do after you score the engagements? You create targeted marketing campaigns to call these high scoring engagements to action. You will have the opportunity to modify the actions you've already specified and 'try again' with a new approach as needed. You may have seen this already with many large-scale marketers. Consider the many ads you see for Coca-Cola for instance. One ad running year after year would fail, even if it scored very well in the first few months.

If you are not already using Google Analytics or another web analytical tool, then you should start soon. Google Analytics starts working nearly immediately to help you determine what traffic is going where. If you scan these reports regularly, you will see where the visitors are engaging your website and from what traffic sources (Facebook post, EventBrite event, Twitter status update, etc.).

Bringing the Team Together

Whichever tools you end up using on whatever platforms for social media, it is important to know that it's highly likely that if you have at least two platforms being used, they probably work together in *some way*. For example, Twitter and Facebook have integration points that allow your Tweets (from one account) to post directly to Facebook new feed just as if the posts originated from Facebook. They come across complete, with a Twitter link (to go back to Twitter and read the original) plus with images and hashtags.

Facebook posts, just like Twitter, go across platforms. The Facebook integration with Twitter allows for an abbreviated version of your public posts to Facebook to be sent to your Twitter stream. The shortened URL from fb will show for the text of your post. People will have to click on the link (the URL with fb) to see the entire post in Facebook. When you're planning on using Facebook integrated with flow to Twitter, you should consider using hashtags (explained in detail later) within the first 140 characters you type in Facebook (because Twitter has a character limit).

The technical aspects of how the various social media platforms integrate, as described with the Twitter-Facebook integration above, are available from the help pages of the respective platform sites (like support.twitter.com).

Plan with your team which integration points would be needed to share the most content (message support) to the most locations possible without recreating content. For example, I often create posts in Facebook that automatically post to Twitter and Google+. Also, this type of integration does involve a few technical steps. A lot of this technical or complex work can be eliminated with a tool such as HootSuite (from hootsuite.com).

I highly recommend HootSuite even though to use it to its best potential is not free (up to 5 streams is allowed in the free account). Take a look at their plans and products after you've used the platforms individually for a while, you will likely appreciate the time savings that HootSuite can afford you. There are other tools like HootSuite. A list of handy social media tools has been provided in the Appendix.

Aspects of Social Media: Twitter

Let's get started with Twitter! Twitter is often misunderstood and people may not appreciate its outreach potential. Because of this, those who use Twitter tend to be more die-hard users and have been able to figure out their niche. Twitter is a micro-blogging service. Imagine it as Blogger or WordPress, condensed to a tiny 140-character limit per post.

Niche usage was mentioned earlier. If you do not target a niche within Twitter, then you're not as likely to gain as many followers (one of the key goals within the use of Twitter as an activist tool). Being a broad-base "Tweeter" will get you followers, but the engagement level is likely to be lower.

I use multiple Twitter accounts: Personal, Campaign, Business and Controversial. I use different accounts because I don't want to mix the messaging among them. Followers for my Business account do not necessarily want to read posts regarding my campaign or political activism. If you plan on using Twitter for activism and you already have a personal account (one you use for communicating with friends, neighbors and family – people who know you in real life), then you should strongly consider opening an account which is purely aligned to the niche you've chosen.

What is Twitter? From Hashtag.org: "The purpose of Twitter is to share information with the public, so if you are a very private person do not want strangers lurking, perhaps a public platform is not for you. Otherwise, you can protect your account, which defeats the very objective of Twitter in the first place."

It is possible, however, to be anonymous on Twitter. You can create Twitter accounts that use a 'pen name' and Tweet whatever comes to mind. You'll have to keep in mind that Tweeting information on your location, job, family and other characteristics may lead people to identify who you really are.

Opening a Twitter Account

Getting started in the basics of Twitter is a breeze. This guide will walk you through the steps. Sometimes, Twitter makes slight changes to their forms and screens (the user interface). This shouldn't greatly affect any information in these steps.

1. Visit URL: http://twitter.com/

New to Twitter? Sign up

Full name

Email

Password

Sign up for Twitter

Twitter 1: Sign up

Enter the Full Name, Email and Password you'd like to use for the account. If you are planning on using the account in an 'anonymous' way, then you can use a Pen Name (see example). Click the "Sign up for Twitter" button to continue.

2. Verify the data shown on the "Join Twitter Today" form. Your entries will be checked for practical use guidelines. If you receive an error, simply make the recommended changes.

3. A User name will be generated for you from your "Full Name". Don't worry about this at this time, you can change it after you set up your account. It is a good idea to change it to fit your Cause though.

   You have the option to select "Keep me signed-in on this Computer" and "Tailor Twitter..." The Tailor option is a good one to choose for those new to Twitter since it will expose you to others who already Tweet. You can learn from their Tweets. When you are ready to continue, you click "Create my Account" - the obscenely large gold button.

4. Twitter will set up your account credentials. When it is done, you will see the Welcome screen. You will follow the steps to choose Timeline entries (people or organizations you want to follow). To do this most effectively, you may wish to search for groups that are already related to your cause. Use the search bar and type the keywords or the group name that relates. Click the magnifying glass and review the results in the results area. When you find any group or person who is worthy of a follow, Click the Follow button.

5. After you have followed at least five in Twitter, you will continue with Twitter forcing you to follow at least five more on the next screen. This screen has Twitter accounts listed based upon a general category. This makes it useful to identify Government, Sports or other figures. When you find a category that would likely contain the accounts you would like to add (for this step), simply click on the category and view the accounts grouped within. Choose follow for each of the accounts until you have at least five. If you can't find five that you really like, you can always add

some and delete them later. Click Next to move along to the next screen.

6. You can choose an email service to import contacts. Unless you have a lot of Cause-based contacts, use the "Skip" option (cleverly hidden with gray text) to continue the process.

7. If you have a logo for the cause (a really a great idea since it is part of your branding), you can use it or a suitable image. The best size is an image crafted in 73x73 pixels in PNG or JPG. The image file will need to be under 700Kb.

8. After the image for your profile is loaded, use the best 160 characters you can to describe your cause while making sure it's catchy. You can always change this later. A good start is ideal since you may forget to come back to this later. Click **Done** when you have finished your Bio entry.

9. You will need to go to your registered email and confirm your account to finalize the activation of your Twitter account. Once this is done, take a look at your Twitter feed!

The screen layout for Twitter is subject to change (don't be surprised if it changes; it changed once during the writing of this book). The layout as of this publication has the summary panel (number of tweets, number of followers and number you are following) along with the Composition field for new tweets. The Timeline or feed for Tweets takes up the most space on the right of the screen. This is a continuous scroll area. The remaining key areas are the 'suggestions' and the current Trends in Twitter.

Occasionally, the suggested Follows are really great. If you follow someone and decide later to drop them, you can do this easily. The Trends are customizable to a

30

general geographic area. For example, you can click "Change" and choose "United States" and "Raleigh" (or your area) to drill down to localized Trending in Twitter.

Remember, you only have 140 characters to make your point. If you eschew using acronyms and text-speak (OMG!), then maybe you will want to resist less with Twitter. Getting your point across can be easier if you can shortcut some words and expressions. Also, you will need to take advantage of Hashtags and the Twitter functions. These will make your Tweets far more effective, increase your followers and help spread your message.

If you want to catch up on the jargon and odd terms used in Twitter, you may want to visit: https://support.twitter.com/articles/166337-the-twitter-glossary

When you're using Twitter, you may find a tweet show up in your stream from someone you are following. It may make you want to say something, not just ReTweet (RT) the original post. This gives you the opportunity to do one of three things that will help you engage more people:

1) ReTweet the original tweet (as mentioned)

2) @Reply to the sender of the original tweet

3) @Mention the sender of the original tweet in your own "new" tweet.

The ReTweet is the simplest and it's essentially just you "copying" the tweet to your followers in Twitter. It's a good practice to edit the tweet and insert "RT" at the beginning of the tweet. Even though Twitter tells your followers that you are ReTweeting, it's a common practice and does give clear credit to the originator.

The @reply is simply a *reply* tweet to the originator (the sender) of the tweet you saw in your stream. Twitter will place their Twitter address (*@originating_person*) in the tweet and you're ready to type the reply. Just leave the @ and their sender info at the start of the tweet box and type away. You still have the 140-character limit.

The @mention is a way to take what they said and run with it. They will see a reply (their @ info will be in the tweet as it starts out as an @reply) along with the new information you type. The best way to do an @mention is simply to hit the reply icon and start typing in the tweet. Move the @address of the person who originated earlier tweet so they are "mentioned" in the new tweet. This way, they are "mentioned". This is a great way to acknowledge their work while engaging them **and** new people.

Some useful tools to employ when using the above techniques are HT, RT and MT. There are others, but these are the most popular. Essentially, RT is, as described earlier, a way to show your followers the information you are ReTweeting is a RT (ReTweet). Place this at the start of the ReTweet and send it. If the tweet yo want to ReTweet needs some modification to suit some other need or length boundary, then you can always MT or Modified Tweet. This is a ReTweet where you've made a change or more to the original. The HT is really a nice way to show people that you appreciate their work from an @mention. People will place HT in the text of a Tweet (not always a ReTweet) before the @ address of the other Twitter user to give them a "Hat Tip" or credit for something they originated. For example:

#CommonCore is getting more of a challenge from #NC parents HT @LadyLiberty1885

Hashtags

A Hashtag is a tag embedded within a Twitter tweet. Think of a hashtag as a keyword for your tweet or for a portion of the content for the tweet. For example, #TarHeel is used in many tweets associated with UNC-CH sports or Alma mater discussions. The Hashtag #Green identifies with the Green Movement.

In the appendix, I have included a list of common activism based hashtags. Also, you should know that most Social Media platforms support hashtags.

Facebook, Twitter, Google+ and Instagram (plus others) use hashtags. When you share a post from one platform to another, the hashtags will work in the new platform just as well!

For really great analytics on hastags (and to actually track your own hashtags), be sure to visit Hashtags.org.

Twitter Functions

Dave Carter @CarterForNC · 15s
I hope that everyone had a safe #MemorialDay. Remember our fallen. Give thanks to the freedoms they have secured for the #USA. #BillofRights

Twitter 3: Tweet with function icons

When you receive tweets from others, they appear in the timeline. The typical tweet will have functions below the actual tweet. This is useful since you can have the tools at your fingertips. In the example above, you see some available in a typical tweet.

The Reply (the little arrow to the left) lets you automatically send a tweet to the sender. The reply tweet will start with the tweeter's @ name. Just type a message and send it. Be sure to make your reply relevant and added value.

Retweet (the arrows forming a circle) automatically sends the original tweet to your followers (posts it to your timeline of Tweets). Essentially, it's a shortcut of copy and send to your friends. This is useful to both you and the person sending the original tweet. Plus, this is vital to the success of your activism campaign in Twitter.

Consider the scenario: You have a twitter account and so does a friend. Your friend has 1000 followers and you have only 500 (but you're working on it!). If you send a Tweet, then 500 people potentially will read it from your followers. (Keep in mind, they have to see it in their timeline. Not all will actually read it.) If your friend retweets the post, then you will have it exposed to your 500 PLUS their 1000 followers. If you're able to make the post 'meaty' enough to get retweeted by more, your exposure can grow geometrically or better. As an activist, it behooves you to get others to Retweet your tweets whenever possible. You need to make sure your social team works hard to get as many followers as possible for each of their accounts. Tweets that you send publicly can be read by anyone, even those who do not follow you.

The *Favorite* tool (small star) gives you a "save for later" option. This is especially handy if you want to hold someone's tweet for later viewing. This is often the case if they included a link (shortcode link, for example) in their tweet. When tweets zip by on the timeline, old tweets will get lost in the shuffle. If you favorite a tweet, you can find it later by visiting the *Me* menu and choosing Favorites. All tweets you "favorited" will appear in a list.

If you originated the tweet, you will have a delete tweet icon as well. This will remove the tweet from your timeline. This is a good tool to keep in mind. If you need to delete a tweet, always try to do it before the tweet gets you into trouble. Many people (Anthony Weiner is one example) have let Twitter be their downfall.

The *More* icon (the ellipsis) shows functions for Emailing the Tweet (for sharing the information with an email user you know) and for embedding the tweet. This is especially handy if you would like to re-use Twitter information with others on your blog or website. One caveat: If the original Tweet is deleted in Twitter, the embed code will reveal an error on your website. Not too bad, but you should check the site frequently for changes. The Pin Tweet tool allows you to lock or "Pin" your tweet to the profile page for your Twitter account. This tweet will replace any other pinned tweet that you may have already had there. A pinned tweet will show at the top of all of your tweets (the history of your tweets) to any user who views your profile.

With regard to the embed tweet – this is an ideal presentation to many people for sharing messages to your followers and to those who frequent your website "hub". The embed code permits the readers of your website to see the tweets (from your cause-based group) embedded in the site's pages. The tweets show their profile pictures, the Twitter address (@) and the functions you can leverage to get others to *follow, retweet, favorite* and *reply* to your tweets. This can be a gold mine, if harnessed well. It's a good idea to have someone somewhat technical help you with the embed tweet function. The HTML that the tweet code provides needs to be placed within the HTML of the webpage that will host the embedded tweet.

Twitter Tools

When using Twitter with multiple accounts, it's often better to utilize a consolidation tool such as TweetDeck or Hootsuite. There is a list of these tools in the appendix. A consolidation tool will allow you to tweet to multiple accounts at once or simply have access to multiple accounts from one screen. This is much simpler than having to log into multiple accounts to send tweets. This is especially useful for anyone who manages Twitter accounts for others.

Another useful function available on many Twitter toolsets is a Tweet-ahead or Tweet scheduling function. With a tool like this, you can type your tweet in advance and load it to a schedule. This means your tweet will be automatically posted to Twitter followers when scheduled. You don't have to live tweet. If you're going to be busy for the next day, but want to make sure that your followers have something from your Twitter account to read, simply schedule a tweet or two in advance.

Twitter Challenge

If you ever hold an event (which should be listed in Facebook and Google+, if you have those accounts), a really great idea is to have people at the event "live tweet" the event. This is a simple way to get others to advertise not only the event, but your campaign or cause. Here's how it's done:

- ✓ Decide upon a hashtag for the event. Let's say it's a park clean up day at a park called "Metro Park". You can have a hashtag of "#ILoveMetroPark".

✓ Before the event, send tweets with that hashtag and include the URL to the website (yours!) that explains the event or why it's important to you. Also send other tweets that lead people to the Facebook event (URL for the event) or other event scheduling tool (like Eventbrite) and include the same hashtag.

✓ At the event, you display a poster board sign that reads, "Live tweet and use hashtag #ILoveMetroPark".

✓ Follow the hashtag (click on the hashtag in your Twitter stream or search for it in the search bar) during the event. Encourage people to tweet photos and always use the hashtag.

✓ After the event, remember to recap with the hashtag to the followers. Consider adding statistics of how many tweets, how many attendees, and more on an article or blog post on your website. Include photos from the event.

Aspects of Social Media: Facebook

Facebook is the behemoth of the Social Media world. Its user base is tremendous. It's marketing potential is also tremendous. If you're not tapping into the exposure available through Facebook, then you are missing out.

I had heard recently that if Twitter is like "speed-dating", then Facebook is like a "Backyard BBQ". Facebook allows you to spend some time with people in more meaningful dialogue than Twitter.

One of the key aspects of Facebook which make it vital to the success of an activism campaign is it's principal demographic: Youth. Understandably, many adults use Facebook too. This is not a youth-exclusive platform. In fact, one of the fastest growing groups on Facebook is the 60+/Female group. Harnessing the power of Facebook is essential.

Joining Facebook is simple. Start out by visiting the site http://www.Facebook.com.

There are a number of steps they will walk you through but they are all simple and don't take much time. No guide is needed since they are fairly simple. Follow the information provided on the screens from Facebook. In no time, you will have a Facebook account and you will be posting your "status updates" to your timeline.

How to leverage Facebook

Many people find Facebook easy to navigate and use for personal social media. It is fairly straightforward for most people. The prompts on the Facebook forms let you know what and where to type.

Facebook is used by most people as a way to showcase their identity. You can use it to showcase your cause and its identity. This is done through the use of the Facebook fan pages. Fan Pages can exist in any of the following categories: Local Business or Place; Company, Organization or Institution; Brand or Product; Artist, Band or Public Figure; Entertainment; or Cause or Community. If you wish to maximize your exposure, you may choose more than one and create pages separately. But, when you are starting out, stick with one fan page type to keep your messaging clear and directed.

As you set up your Facebook fan page for the cause (or community), you will need to provide some key information and data to the set-up process. Gather a great description for your fan page. Get some photos or images related to the page. Two of these will be used immediately for your Profile photo and your cover photo. Other photos should be added to the photo albums for your Fan Page. Why? People are curious and love to look at photo albums.

For the set-up process, you will be asked to upload a profile photo (image). The ideal image is one that will help convey the mission or the message to the readers and the general audience of the fan page. Recall that the page is a way to showcase your identity. Let's look at this as a way to help people relate and want to relate to the group or cause. For example, the image should allow for easy identification of the cause or group. Someone who creates a page for Firemen Appreciation, for example, could have a photo of a group of firemen in front of a fire or a pumper truck. This is a readily identifiable image. This is key since all posts provided will have a miniature version of this profile image presented alongside the content. It's constant re-branding.

The Cover image for Facebook (in the current mode of Facebook) is a 850x315 pixel image. You can have a bigger picture, but you will have to do some image manipulation to get the image you want. You are better off creating an image in a photo-editing tool (such as PhotoShop or similar) which gives you a resulting image sized 850px x 315px. This will ensure that your graphics are not altered by Facebook at all. This also allows you to embed a very small amount of text along with your image. Facebook does not allow you to have a large amount of text in your cover image. This is fine for most organizations since you can easily convey a message well with images. Many cover images are composite images such as a mosaic of images or a tiled group of images. For whichever style you choose, understand that the lower left portion of the image is likely to be covered by the overlapped Profile image. Clever photo image editing can leave a nice space for the profile image on the cover image.

After you complete the set-up steps for the Facebook fan page. You will need to click on the Change Cover (or Add Cover) link on the upper image area of the Fan page. Upload the cover image you created and you're set. Take a look at the Coca-Cola example below for an idea of what the end result can be. Think of this set of images as a billboard (limit the text!) for your cause.

Important Nugget

This is a great tip for anyone wishing to increase their community engagement. In fact, this should have neon surrounding this to bring it out to everyone.

Remember to tag people in photos.

It's simple, I know. But it is powerful. Let's say you have a photograph of a bunch of college volunteers for your cause. Be sure to tag (you need to make sure these people are your friends – or have someone who has them as a friend do this) at least a couple of people in any group shot. The reason for this: They will have this photograph show on their news feed. That means their friends see it. They, will probably like it. Maybe they will tag someone. See how this goes? It will spread.

What you will end up posting is a solid bit of text along with a photograph. The text may have some great hashtags (to lead people to click on them and investigate further) along with (perhaps) a link to a key website article. The photograph will have some tags. *Plus*, you can invite people in the post itself with: "Feel free to tag your friends in this photograph." Instant engagement, right?

Engagement in Facebook

Facebook 1: Sample Cover Image for a Page

With Facebook, you are in control of your messaging. You will be able to engage others in the continuation of the message. Involving others through your social media network is simple with Facebook. Each person in the network can share and like the posts to the Fan page you create. Supporters for the cause who are part of the social media team should be the first to share the page's posts and like them. Comments on posts also will engage others to get involved, comment, share, and *like*.

You should use the status updates carefully. Keep strategy in mind as you post. Posts to the status such as important happenings, events, and similar are needed. Fill in the status with advice and commentary on issues related to the cause. Don't be afraid to use the tools mentioned in other areas of this book. Getting engagement is vital to spreading of your message via Facebook. If engagement occurs, then you will find the sharing, *liking* and network expansion increasing. Your posts will set the identity of the cause. Some can be (and should be) lighthearted. Humor will attract readers and fans. Photos do the same. Be sure that you continue posting (and frequently post!) information that underscores the identity of your organization.

There is a free tool (it's free because they embed their ad in anything they do) that is wonderful for creating customized and professional timeline cover photos. Pagemodo.com offers numerous attractive options for free. If you're pressed for time and don't want to spend a lot of time editing photos and graphics, then this is a great option for you.

As of the time of this writing, Facebook was beginning their beta rollout of their new Facebook pages. The new format is only slightly different from the current format. Most notably, the branding for the page is more apparent in the new version.

Facebook Events

Facebook events are wonderful tools to build attendance for functions and events you may hold. Even small events like a team meeting (that you don't mind sharing with the public) can be used to gain attention for your cause.

With a new event in Facebook, you get options that will allow you to not only target the default 'users' (people who have liked your page) but you can promote your event specific users with select targeting.

The "Where" field will allow you to embed a "place" from Facebook (especially useful if people like to Check-

In) or a simple address. The Tickets field will accept a URL from Eventbrite or similar online event management system.

Remember to remind the participants in the events to tag the event (check-in as well) to increase your visibility.

Key Considerations with Facebook

Facebook will allow you to create either a group for a campaign or cause or a Fan Page. I covered Fan Pages specifically because it has strengths over the use of a group. By all means, you can and perhaps should use a Facebook Group too if you would like to promote Facebook based communications within your group (team/network). Facebook Groups have some benefits worth of mention: Group messaging, file storage and integrated events (tab) within the *group* page. Facebook Fan Pages, however, have a clear advantage if you have technical resources at your disposal. With the use of HTML, JavaScript and CSS and the ability to set a designated landing tab you can capture your inbound audience and lead them exactly to the spot you need them to begin. Plus, you can do this with the look and feel you want and expect for your campaign. If you use the technologies indicated you can follow a process very similar to setting up separate pages on a website. You can build tabs for information on the issue or cause or candidate, forms for volunteer sign-ups, and setting up a welcome page for people new to the Facebook experience for your cause/campaign.

Facebook Insights is a tool that is available for your Facebook page that gives valuable data points:

1. Total Likes
2. Friends of Fans

3. People Talking about This

4. Weekly Total Reach

5. Visits

6. When fans are online (for Post reach)

To access Insights for your Facebook page, look for the following menu at the top of your Facebook page:

| Edit Page ▼ | Build Audience ▼ | See Insights | Help ▼ |

Facebook 2: Facebook Insights Menu

The Overview tab from Insights gives you 'at-a-glance' data that can help with quick decisions for the effectiveness of a campaign within 24 hours of campaign post deployment. Page Likes are clearly displayed and help you see when the Likes occurred with consideration of week over week comparison points. For instance, if you launched a new facet of your campaign that included new posts this week and there were no posts last week, you will be able to see whether the Likes (possibly attributable to the posts and reader engagement) have increased (or decreased). In the example below, we see that the page Likes increased only 1.2% week over week. The prior week is displayed in a lighter format behind the current week's graph of Likes. You will also see the page's total Likes.

Post reach gives you a cumulative view of how many people viewed (and hopefully read,) your posts. This is especially handy to determine how your posts are performing over time.

Facebook 3: Insights overview

The Engagement view describes *how* people are engaged with your content. This should be key for you. The overall "People Engaged" metric tells you how many people were engaged with your page over the course of that time frame (dates are included). You should always see an upward trend while you are in your Page building mode. When your Page is more mature, a positive number is still great but cannot always be expected. The week over week comparison will let you know how your week's posts are engaging people. It is possible that one of your older posts gets recycled by someone Liking or Commenting, but the majority of post engagement is typically more recent (this week). Engagements of Like, Comments and Shares are vital to growing your presence within the Facebook universe. These metrics, especially Comments and Shares, are important to follow. *Post* clicks are important to determining whether people (and how many) are engaging "through" your post. For example, you created some content on your website. You then took the URL from your website and posted it within your Facebook page for your organization. After a week, you can see the Post Clicks (in the overview mode, this is for all posts) that can be attributed to your website link. If you are using Google Analytics, this number (for the specific post or for the site in general) should be very close to the sourced visits from Facebook.

Facebook Insights, like Google Analytics, can be a treasure trove of data for analysis. Don't get too bogged down in the data as you use it. Sometimes it's possible to 'over analyze' when all you need to see is whether a particular post is reaching a broad audience.

Be sure to take time to investigate all aspects of the Facebook Insights views since there are far more useful data points than what I provided in this summary.

Aspects of Social Media:YouTube

Many people do not think of YouTube as a Social media site or tool. They may be missing out on the possible audience available to them. If you think about it, YouTube has become as common to us as Google. People use the word YouTube as a verb now: "YouTube the term Social Media." It's a fact that YouTube is the second largest search engine in the world (behind Google).

Since YouTube allows audience members to comment (if comments are allowed by the account) on a video, they engage a social audience to act. If you present a solid message in a video, get commentary that is positive, people will be swayed. Why? Remember, 90% of the people are more likely to believe peer recommendation and only 14% trust advertisements. Your YouTube can be your advertisements which are believable to people.

YouTube works most effectively if you have a channel and can control the video on your channel. This means you have the means distribute the video content that not only supports the cause, but also informs and entertains your audience. Setting up a channel is simple and should be done from an email account that can be shared. This email account will be the login account for the YouTube channel (and other Google Services).

Getting Started with a Channel

If you already have a Google.com account (Gmail, Google API, Maps, or other Google empire log in), then you are already on your way to establishing an account for a YouTube channel. If you'd like to share the responsibility for YouTube channel management with others, then it's a good idea to create a new "Shared" Google.com account which will be useful for others to share (password and content).

If you don't have an account with Google.com, you will be forced to create one before you set up your YouTube channel. You may want to coordinate this with the team who may be using Google for email (shared) and GooglePlus (Google+).

Log in to the Google account and head over to the YouTube site (http://www.Youtube.com). Notice the link for creating a new YouTube account. Click here and follow the steps (Google likes to move things around from time to time – this is why we do not have an image of the process here).

In creating a YouTube channel name, keep in mind the following characteristics:

- ⋏ Create a strong and memorable "brand" of your own

- ⋏ Keep it short AND memorable ("AgainstMeat" is better than "PeopleWhoPromoteVegan")

- ⋏ Stick with your image. Are you all about local water? Are you about social causes? Supporters of micro-brews?

- ⋏ Use Mixed caps (also called Camel-back): "ProperCaseMixedWithoutSpaces" to make it easy to read since you can't use spaces in the User-name for the Channel.

Once you've set up the User Name and related information, you will need to customize the channel. You can find the link for "My Channel" and "Channel

Settings". On the Appearance tab, add your organization's logo or Avatar (800x800 pixels and 1 Mb max). This is especially important since your avatar will be visible with all videos you post. Tweak the color scheme to match your branding colors. Choose a background image to help show off your branding and your videos as they appear on you channel. If you're unfamiliar with a background image, imagine a scrap book with a colorful background to the photos. This is what the channel background will be like. You will need to choose whether this image is tiled (repeated) horizontally, vertically, or both. Another option is to "not repeat". This option locks the image into the center of the channel page's background. If you choose the "scrolling" option (contrast with "fixed"), the image will move downward as your viewers scroll down (such as moving down a list of videos). This keeps the image constantly visible. Experiment with the options for the background until you find the optimum blend of placement and layout for your background Branding.

The new layout for YouTube (2013 offering) includes the background (banner) image (Recommended channel art size: 2120 x 1192 pixels). This is similar to the layout that is provided by Facebook with their banner-style image. The inset image is 800x800px (formerly, the Avatar image). The banner has different aspects for different devices. The best possible size for your channel art is 2560x1440px. However, if you use this size, you should use a channel art template (see appendix for location of useful templates). Use the tool provided by YouTube to test the view on each of the device platforms before you finalize your art. It will take a few iterations to make the best fit work for all devices. It will be worth it.

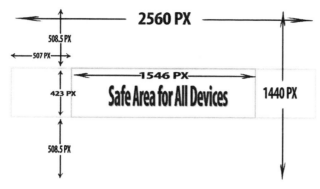

YouTube 1: Channel Art sample Template

On the Info and Settings tab, give the Channel a good title. This is not the channel name. But, this name will appear at the top of many of your channel's pages. Keep it catchy and stick to your branding. Use the old NY Times' branding "All the News That's Fit to Print" as an example of what could go in a Title. The Description field is vital for good information. This gives your organization's mission or public facing statement that will help others understand more about you. Be sure to use "http://www.whateveryourwebsiteis.com" (not literally, just replace the text above with your home page URL) in the description. This will give your viewers a link to go to your organization's home page.

When it comes to setting your Tags, use a lot of the same words you used in your description. For example, if your description is: "We establish security for something and do things for someone." (generic enough for you?) Then your tags can be something like: *Security establish something*. The words don't have to make a sentence. The words should be "Keywords" which describe your organization and its mission.

You will want to take note of your Channel's URL. This URL will be your key to distribution of your message. Use this URL in your Tweets about your videos and Facebook status updates about content in YouTube.

Metadata is the information such as the keywords, title and video description you've entered. If you optimize this metadata, it will improve your channel and subsequently your videos' search returns. Ideally, both Google and YouTube will rank your videos higher based upon the data you place within the metadata.

I've learned this from trial and error. You can see the results by testing this yourself. Do a search for your keywords in both Google and YouTube. Make a note of what page(s) the target video(s) show. Then, make changes to your metadata and save the changes. Google will update the keywords and related metadata fairly quickly. After an hour, test your search within YouTube and Google. Did your videos drop in rankings? Did they move to a better page? Repeat this process until you see the returned hits as close to page one or on page one for your search terms.

Here are some tips to follow for your metadata:

- Use the best title (and correct title) for your video

- Use the tags (keywords) fully.

- Use a great video description.

- Use your URL at the beginning of every video description.

- Use some of your keywords (tags) in your description as well.

One thing I learned from a 'guru' in YouTube is to use tags that are "opposite" of your subject. Let's make this easier to comprehend with an example. You have a video for a candidate that you are promoting on your channel. The candidate's name is Calvin Coolidge. Richard Long is the opponent. When you tag the video, it's a good idea to use the opponent's name, "Richard Long", as a tag as well as your candidate's name, "Calvin Coolidge". You'd do this for any candidate's campaign. You'd also consider this technique for any cause video.

Working with your Channel

Creating the YouTube channel is the easy part. Populating this is harder. Uploading videos is actually easy. Getting them filmed and edited is tough. Once you have them, upload them to YouTube and share them via other social media outlets.

Once videos are loaded (even if you just load one), start using the social media tools embedded within the channel and on YouTube to share with others.

YouTube 2: YouTube Channel

In the example channel above, the About 'tab' is active (underlined word "About"). You can see in the view that the channel's video has 12 views and no likes or dislikes (the up and down icons). You can use the

'Channel settings' button to quickly navigate to the settings for your whole channel (useful for changing the layout or colors when your branding needs a touch up).

The Share tab (next to About) is very important. This is where you get to the meat of social media interaction driving. Creating the content (whether it's a video, blog or Facebook content) is the first step. Driving interactions is key for your activism. You can increase your stickiness (amount of time a user spends reading or viewing your content) by increasing the amount of quality content and by sharing it broadly.

YouTube 3: Sharing a video

Click on the Share tab and you will see the sharing options from your video. Click on the right arrow button and you will see all available sharing platforms.

http://youtu.be/rfSGoad9yqM

YouTube 4: Sharing destinations for YouTube videos

Let's cover these and some of their applications. First, the shortened URL (youtu.be...) is very handy to send your video's link to others via email without the longer link. This is especially handy with link sensitive devices (and apps) such as mobile phone (text messages) and Twitter messages. Simply cut and paste the shortened URL or retype it (case is key here!) on your mobile phone for a text message to someone.

The icons across this image (left to right) are as follows:

[f]	Facebook	
	Twitter	[y]
[g+]	Google+	
	Tumblr	[t]
[P]	Pinterest	
	Blogger	[B]
[Su]	StumbleUpon	
	LinkedIn	[in]
[my]	MySpace	
	Reddit	[Reddit icon]

These icons and sharing links may change from time to time (the social media world is constantly on the move), so this reference may be obsolete or in need of alteration by the time you read this.

For the most part, you should stick with the first three or four (Facebook, Twitter, Google+ and Tumblr) as a *minimum* for your social media activism. Since Google's YouTube gives you the tools at your fingertips, use them whenever you can. For example, to Tweet this video, you will click on the Twitter icon and YouTube will request for you to log into Twitter (only if you are not already logged in on the same computer). When you're logged in, it will give you a sample of what it will Tweet on your behalf. You can change this text (but don't change the URL!) as you need to craft your message further. You will still need to keep an eye on the remaining characters allowed (Twitter's limitation). When you're ready, click the Tweet button. Your Tweet will include a link to the video for all of your Twitter followers to enjoy. Plus, this Tweet, if re-Tweeted, will be shared with countless others who may, also, view your video. Again, it's viral marketing for your cause.

As long as you stick to a consistent message (based upon your campaign), you can use any of the social media and other sharing tools available from YouTube. You can also reach beyond these (as mentioned with the email or text messaging options just using the short URL) to significantly expand your reach.

Continuing with YouTube

Since YouTube offers you video content, you should work to prepare your own content as well as sharing content created by others. If you have content from others, you can add this to your Channel playlist (name your playlist accordingly). This playlist will be available to others who may subscribe to your Channel. Ideally, everyone who receives your messaging will subscribe to your Channel. This ensures that new content will be shared with them as it's released.

To create and update Playlists:

1. Click Video Manager in your YouTube menu (upper right of your YouTube screen when you are already logged in to YouTube).

2. Click on the Playlists option under the Video Manager menu

3. Click on the check box for the playlist you would like to edit and click Edit (button) or click the +New Playlist button to create a new playlist.

4. You should set the Title of the playlist (public will see this title, make it clear and concise) along with the Description. You have 5000 characters for the Description. Take advantage of this. Search Engines can find this information and lead more people to you and your cause.

5. Choose the Privacy and other Settings for the Playlist and click the Save button. This will set your playlist up and make it available.

6. Add videos to your playlist (as you edit the Playlist) which will support (1) Your Channel and (2) the Playlist title and mission.

If you promote your Channel like you promote your videos, you will find that the subscriptions will increase for your channel and your message reach will increase with it.

YouTube is a must to distribute the content that is able to speak for itself. Snippets of public meetings, shorts from public or government released videos and custom shot pieces are very effective when placed not only in your hub site (website) for your cause, but in each of the spoke sites: A link to a video in Twitter or Google+, another upload with a link within Facebook, an upload in Vimeo with a link to home page, and a detailed description (and perhaps even a transcript of the video) on the home page. Since YouTube is one of the highest rated SEO sites (well, Google does own them), you're going to miss out on increasing your audience if you do not take advantage of the video platform to promote your cause. Even if you do not have access to a video camera or editing software, the YouTube tools for videos will allow you to take advantage of the simple uploads you can provide from an iPad, iPhone or Android phone. The tools and enhancements available can make you video ready in minutes even if you're capturing key video out "in the field". The immediate gratification available with YouTube can make it easier for you to capture the attention of possible activists who will join your team.

Your Social Media shares of YouTube videos should bring people to view your playlists and videos more. You will also want to drive (use a call to action, when possible) people to "Subscribe" to your channel. This is a simple function and if you provide solid content, people will do this.

One of the best YouTube-based activism programs was released by Amnesty International in response to violations of human rights. Take a look at the power of video: http://youtu.be/R5c_C9Ug_J8

YouTube One Channel

YouTube, in 2013, released their latest update. The new features really allow for you to have your channel increase its impressions. Here is a quick review of some of the important impacts:

1) Trailer video (only appears to non-subscribed viewers). This will help you snag new viewers AND subscribers

2) Image and branding setup for your channel will now port to all devices (such as smartphones using mobile YouTube).

3) Organizing your playlist and channel is easier and has more impact.

YouTube Special Considerations

According to Heyo, 52% of video content (online) happens through Social Media. This means that harnessing video to reach your community is more important as people are using video more than ever before.

Vimeo and Vine

Vimeo and Vine are also video-related platforms that should not be ignored. Vimeo is much smaller than YouTube. But that doesn't make YouTube better. YouTube doesn't have the professional appeal that Vimeo has. It's also considered to be a little more hip than YouTube.

Vine, now owned by Twitter, gives you the ability to load six-second video clips to a social sharing stream. Think of this as the Twitter version of YouTube. The videos are compact and really should get to the point quickly. It's perfect for the short attention spans we find.

Aspects of Social Media: Google+

Google didn't stay out of the Social Media fray for very long. While Facebook and MySpace defined the markeplace, Google was definining search engine tools, web management and more. They also had a team making sure they had a competitive offering in social media.

Google+ is not considered by many to be a strong competitor to Facebook. However, most people also overlook its natural reach. Consider this: Google will promote it's "own" customers first. Have you thought about how large the search engine usage is for Google alone? Let's consider another example: Google wholly owns YouTube. Did you know that YouTube is in the top 5 of all search *engines* in use today? While Google+ for social media sharing may not be top dog, but it is something you cannot ignore if you want to build the biggest presence with a small team.

Getting Started with Google+

Google+ requires that you have a Google account of some sort to begin. If you already have setup Gmail or your YouTube account, then you already have a starting point for your Google+ account. A suggestion worth repeating: Have an account that can be shared for your social media team and do not use a private email (Gmail) account. This gives your team access to YouTube and Google+ from the same log in. This also allows for faster sharing of content across platforms.

If you do not already have a Google account, create one now at Google.com. To get started with Google+, locate the + in the upper corner of the Google main screen (such as the search screen) and click it (or just visit the site http://plus.google.com). In many cases, the +You is the Google+ link.

Once you access Google+, it can be a bit confusing as to what you can and should do. This is one of the key detractors from Google+ as compared to Facebook and even Twitter. Don't let this discourage you from using it. It is very powerful for social media sharing.

Using Google+

Circles are the key aspect of Google+. These give you the power to share and share broadly. Building your circles is similar to adding friends in Facebook and followers in Twitter. It may take time to build your circles, but it doesn't have to. Take advantage of your existing contacts (email and otherwise) and share with them that you are on Google+.

Circles allow you to choose any or all groups (circles) to share information. It can be a Family circle for recipes, a Co-Workers circle for jokes at work, and a Friends circle for local event information. Your circles are customizable and you can create as many as you need to manage your contacts for sharing.

If you do not have any people in your "circles", it's no problem. Google makes it easy to add people to your circles and to create new circles on the fly.

The menu labeled Home from Google+ has many submenus. Use the People option to locate people from your work, your school, your groups (such as Chambers of Commerce, Clubs, and other civic organizations) and other current and former associations. This is vital to creating a large list of populated circles. Let's consider an example of how to build a large group of populated circles.

Google+ 1: Finding People and others to add to Circles

You have many choices in searching for people and entities to add to your Google Circles. The handy search function from within the People screen is a start.

First, make a list of all groups you are part of:

⋏ Work (past and current) and work affiliations

⋏ Schools (past and current)

⋏ Clubs

⋏ Church/Religious Groups

⋏ Previous cities/neighborhoods (you will be surprised how many circles can be made for former neighborhoods and locales)

Now, use Google+ with each that you have identified and add people (Google will help you identify people who may already be in that group) to your circles. Simply use the search function to locate them.

This process may be easier for you if you took extra time when setting up the Education, Work and other aspects of the "About" section of the Profile under Google+. This is because Google will automatically help you create circles for your former organizations.

Once you have a population of circles filled with contacts, you are set and ready to go with the fun parts of Google+.

Making Google+ a Social Media Marvel

The Home of Google+ is your status stream. You will see posts both by you and by people in your circles. This is very similar to the Wall or News Feed of Facebook. When you share on Google+, your content is added to your Home page and to the Home pages of people you shared with who have you in their circles.

As you view the status messages in your stream, you can contribute to the message by commenting, liking - Plus (+1), and sharing the status. The +1 is to "like" the post in the stream. The little arrow swoosh is to share the post with others. Plus, you can see the "Add a comment..." field in the post. When you contribute to meaningful posts – you create engagement. Remember, engagement will bring people into the conversation even if they are lurking on the sidelines.

To create and share a post:

1. Click Share what's new in the share box at the top of your home page or + Share in the Google bar in the upper right.

2. Enter your information to share (this is also called a post). Click on the miniature camera to add a photo, the YouTube play button to add a video, the calendar icon to add an event, or the chain link to add a link (a website or handy bit of content from the web).

Click + Add more people then select a circle or type the name of individual people you'd like to share your post with. You might see a pre-populated group of people already in the box. If you'd like to remove a circle or person, click the X next to their name.

You should keep in mind that many shared posts become available to search engines. For you, this is very handy. For those who wish to remain secretive, this is not a good feature. It's good to share things for your cause. Be loud and in public with the posts. You can share with your circles (and search engines) to build exposure for your cause.

You can also *lock* (now called "disable reshares") your post or *disable comments* by clicking the arrow in the right of the + Add more people box. When you are ready to send the post, click the Share button.

Google+ 2: A Post

> You can use Hashtags within Google Plus to make your posts stand out.

Making your Posts Special

If you note from the example above, you <u>can</u> use formatting inside of posts for Google+. You cannot do this (as of this publication) within Twitter or Facebook. Here's a simple list of formatting tips which will help you make your posts stand out among the many posts in the streams:

Strikethrough: Use the – symbol to surround the word to be struck. Example
-error- becomes ~~error~~

Italic: Use the _ symbol to surround the word to be italicized. Example _amazing_ becomes *amazing*.

Bold: Use the * symbol to surround the word to be bolded. Example *Don't * becomes **Don't**.

Google+ 3: Formatted Post

Google+ 4: Final Result of Formatting and Hashtags added

Getting Paged

If you have already set up your "personal" Gmail account for your cause, then you have a "personal" profile that you are using for Google+ (provided you've already started experimenting with it from the information provided in this guide.) This is great.

When you've built the expertise you need to step into the Google+ world fully for your organization, then you should create the Google+ Page for your group. This is a powerful SEO tool for your organization. In addition, you can use Google Hangouts for your group to create Live Events online for people to attend. They can view video, see your screen and read your information instantly via the Hangout.

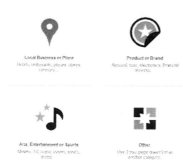

Google+ 5: Types of Pages available in Google+

To set up a page within Google+, determine which category you will use. Most causes and campaigns would use the Company, Institution or Organization type. Some may use Other as their starting point. If you choose the former (Company, Institution or Organization), then you will see a categorny list that includes such choices as "Non-profit" and "Political Organization". Choose the most appropriate for your group and click Next.

Choose a name for your Page. The name should match the name of your organization or cause. If you have a website, include the (URL) address in the field provided. The remainder of the information for setting up your Google+ Page is fairly straightforward. If you've already designed your Facebook page, then much of the information on that can be simply "cut and pasted" into the appropriate fields in Google+.

When the Google+ Page has been created, it's a good idea to add others (on your team) as managers so they can contribute or edit the page as needed. To do this make sure you are viewing the page. If you are not, you can navigate to the page manager by going first to Google+ (plus.google.com) then choosing Pages from the Home menu (on the upper left of screen. If you have more than one page that you manage, you will see them all listed. Click the "Manage this page" button of the desired page to switch to that page in management mode (called the Dashboard). From this view, you will see a tab listing all managers for the page. Click the "View all managers" link. At this point, you should see a button labeled "Add managers".

Each of the managers for a Google+ page must have a Google account. If they already have a Google+ account, they will be notified that they have been added as a manager as soon as you choose to invite them.

Invite new managers

Invite people to help manage this page and any Google products that are connected to it, such as a YouTube channel. Also, choose a role for them. Learn more about managers and roles.

＋ Add names or email addresses

Manager ˅   Cancel   Invite

Google+ 6: Adding Managers to a Google+ Page

There are two options for the Google+ managers: Manager and Communications Manager. There is a third, but that the person who created the page already took that title. This person is known as the "Owner". A owner has all rights to all functions of a page. The Managers have rights to edit the profile, manage YouTube videos added to the account, start and manage Google Hangouts and most other actions. The *Communication Manager* has the authorization to do most of the other actions. This would include adding posts, photos, videos, links and related communications-related activities on the page.

It is possible to transfer ownership of a page. To do this, the non-owner must also be a manager first. From the same managers screen (as you discovered above), locate the existing manager who will become the new owner. Click the down arrow and select "Transfer ownership to…" Once you complete this process, the new owner information will be recorded for the Page and the former owner will become a manager.

Google+ 7: Setting Manager Type

There are other key settings that you should investigate as you work with your Google+ Page. Visit the Home menu and choose the Settings option. Most of the settings here are fairly self-explanatory or have "Learn more" options that you can click on for more information. I will revisit some of the more advanced settings in here in the Appendix.

Click on the "For your site" menu option for the Settings. If you're a more technical user, these tools are very handy to integrate Google+ with your cause's website. Work with your webmaster to get the **+1** button, the Badge, Sharing and the Google Snippet turned on in the best locations for your website.

Embedding Posts

As you develop high quality posts (social media posts) within Google+, you can share the content *back* to your website. One of the most effective, and powerful ways to share content between your website and Google+ is to actually embed the Google+ post on your website.

Start out by creating a post within Google+ so it is visible to the Public. Once posted, revisit the post and click on the down arrow menu (drop down menu) on the upper right of the post. Click "Embed post" from this menu. Copy the HTML given and follow the simple instructions to paste this into your website. The resulting widget will appear on your website where you'd like it to appear and it will be formatted to appear much like it would within Google+. It will also retain the dynamic linking back to your original post.

Google+ Stories

Google has introduced Stories that allow you to "automatically weave your photos, videos and the places you visited into a beautiful travelogue." It also includes a YouTube channel link-through. How this can be used for a campaign or cause remains to be seen. However, it may be a good idea for an enterprising candidate to explore the use of this. Stories are automatically created when users back up their photos from their phones to Google+.

Expanding your Reach

Since Google+ is so easy to get going, it's a wonderful tool to implement to build a broader community for engagement. In fact, Google+ has a "Communities" function that helps you expand and communicate with your relationships.

From the Home menu, choose Communities. You will see "All communities" and "Recommended for you" as options. In addition, you will find Communities you've joined (if any) in buttons at the top of your screen. There is also a search function for communities. This search is often the best starting point for you as you can search for related, like-minded groups that may already exist and join them. However, if you are going to drive your mission's messaging most effectively, you will need to create your own community.

Click the blue button labeled "Create community" on the right of the screen (near the search button). Select Public (you may also make a private community). The private communities are very useful for communicating "opt-in" types of posts and messages. This means that it's not a dialogue with everyone except for those who are invited to be part of the group and have some interest. Either choice is useful (public or private) and the choice of Public here is because this option allows for members to share the content posted in the community with their Circles within Google+. This is important because it allows for your messaging to not only reach your followers (in your Community), but it can be spread outside to the rest of the Google+ universe. Create a Private community if you do not want the content to be spread and only shared within the confines of the community itself.

The Community is a great place to generate dialogues among the members. Think of it as a public forum (for the members, whether private or Public).

Give your community a name and set the basic preferences. You will need to load a photo or image to represent your group (must be minimum of 250px square). When loading a photo or image for your group, be sure the image is a square (I set mine to 445x445px) and note that the middle portion (viewed vertically) is always visible.

You should also set the tagline for your group. If this is for a campaign, it may be the Campaign's tagline or short messaging. Something like "More Freedom, Less Government" can be used. The remaining setup step is to add information to the "About this community." Enter the information here before you click Done. This information can be changed later, but try to get it set up early so your early adopters will have something to read about the community when they join. This can be a modified version of your "About" text for your Facebook Page or your Google+ Page. Try to add specifics as to what the participants in the community are to do and share.

Now that you've created a Community in Google+, it's time to get it populated. Google+ will walk you through the initial post steps. This will have you invite the public (always a good idea) and people in your existing circles to join the Community. At any time, you can also invite more people to join the Community by clicking the Invite people button on the "About this community" section. This is similar to the original share that Google+ guides you through. It's useful since it helps you capture new people and groups that you may have added to your Circles since the last invitation. Also, it can be used for members of the community to reach out to the people in their respective Circles (essentially, sharing the love of the community).

About this community

Invite people   Share this community

Google+ 8: Invite people to join

As with any other Social Media tool, the Community is only as good as the time you and your team put into it. It's vital to send personal invites to people you have in Google+ and in email lists. If you are a part of larger Communities and Circles in Google+ you can also share this Invitation (like sharing the announcement) with them. You want to build interest and the community membership. You don't want to be a creator of spam mails. Do this process carefully – but do it!

A handy shortcut menu from the main page of the Community (you'll see this page when you navigate to the Community from your Google+ Page home menu) gives you access to the sharing and invitations at any time.

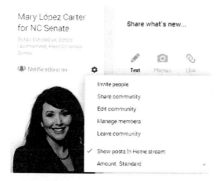

Google+ 9: Shortcut menu (Gear icon) for Community

Remind people in other social media sites (post to your Facebook Page or Group the URL with the long number, it will show wonderfully in Facebook, even though it looks horrendous) of your Community. On your website, embed a badge from Google+ for the Community and urge people to join (this requires some technical expertise but it fairly simple if you have HTML editing skills). You will find that some Facebook members will join your Google+ Community while others, who aren't in Facebook, may join the community as their only option.

When you promote the community (this idea also works within Facebook Groups), if you give the impression that it's "Special" to join or somewhat exclusive, it often motivates or incentivizes people. You don't have to be exclusive, just the air of it often attracts people. This technique works best on a Private or Closed Community but can work on a normal Public Community. In Google + activate the "ask to join" feature if you have a public community.

Once you have the Community running, it's up to you to keep it alive and vibrant. Engagement is what is required to keep folks posting and interested in the content you post. Comments should be encouraged. Sharing should be the norm. Consider using memes and photographs (very common shared items) in your posts. Load posts with articles (summarize the articles to make them easier for people to scan through quickly), links for useful topics and articles, and share other content with the members. Managing a Community can be time-consuming, but it can provide a needed gateway for your activists to share information among themselves and with others.

Events in Google+

From both the Communities and the regular Google+ page, you can create Events to communicate and advertise to others about an upcoming event. The event function has a very attractive theme chooser (to change the graphic banner for the top of the event details) along with the normal fields of Title, date, time and the like.

Google+ 10: Adding a Basic Event

If you'd like some flexibility with the information you'd like to include with the event, Google+ gives you a lot more options under the "Event options" menu. Simply checkmark "Show more options". This will open fields for Website, ticket purchase info (such as Eventbrite or PayPal) and even travel/parking info.

Google+ 11: More details in Event

With the Community Event, you cannot send the event to others using the To field. The event will automatically be "To" the community. With a page event, the To field is editable and allows you to insert any circle, name or email address you'd like for an invitation to the event.

Hanging Out in Google Land

One of the coolest features of Google+ is the Hangout feature.

The Google Hangout is a way to gather people in a forum to share instantly – Screens, videos, Conversations, documents and more.

If you're accustomed to using a tool such as GoToMeeting, then Hangouts are easy for you. If you've never shared your screen in a "webinar" then you're in for a treat with Hangouts from Google.

As a Moderator, you can share a prepared and loaded YouTube video to kick off a meeting. You can then use a Google Drive (storage) document that shows the meeting agenda. Then you can use the Chat window (see appendix for chat commands from Hangout).

As the meeting moves along, you can capture images of the screen (for posterity, note-taking or evidence). Usage of the Screen sharing allows for you to share an individual window (application) on your PC or the entire desktop of your PC. Look here for more: http://youtu.be/7qlunRCjZ2U

While Hangouts may not seem to be readily useful for promoting your cause, if you think outside the box you can explore a lot more. Use Hangouts for your team meetings. Then, use them for small activist presentations to introduce new material or campaigns to people in your circles. Think of hangouts as "easy to get to" meetings and events. People are more inclined to learn more about your cause if it's easy for them to get the information.

Google has expanded the flexibility of Hangouts so that they are cross-platform and readily available. You can start a Hangout on your desktop PC and switch to a mobile phone during the Hangout. Hangouts also works on iPad/iPod.

Hangouts can be private or public. The power of a public Hangout is the involvement of others outside of your normal community. If you have a hot topic, it may help to broadcast the Hangout and let the public know about it to build excitement and attendance.

To initiate a Hangout, you can go on the air with the Hangout function from the Google+ Home menu. Simply choose Hangouts and click the blue button labeled "Start a Hangout On Air." A similar screen to the one shown below will be displayed.

Google+ 12: Public Hangout setup

If you're using a Public Hangout, try to allow enough time for Google to market the event. This will help secure more visitors during the event. If you do an instant Hangout (choosing the Now option instead of scheduling the Hangout with Later), you will have to be sure to invite the specific people for the Hangout to attend. You do the invitations for the Now and the Later options in the Audience section.

If you choose to do an instant hangout with your team, you may also choose to use the "Video Hangouts" option from the Hangouts menu. This will initiate an instant video Hangout with the invited participants. It's a good idea to use the "Include a message" since the participants will be notified of the hangout with the information in the message. The recipients of the Hangout notification will have the Link shared with them. This is a very handy tool since they can tap on the link from their smartphone (equipped with a camera) or click on it from their desktop PC or Mac to launch the Video Hangout.

Google+ 13: Video Hangout setup

Hangouts that you initiate don't have to use video, even though it is a very useful tool. If you initiate a Video hangout and you or a participant doesn't have video capability (or is shy), then they can remain in the hangout using their PC's microphone or their smartphone connection.

Once the Hangout is initiated, you can still add people to the hangout, mute your call, turn video sharing on or off, plus other options. To make the Hangout more engaging, you have the choice of many tools (see image to right). You can start Google Effects (fun tool, mainly –

add hats to the video participants, as an example), open a chat window (very useful during calls that have some limitation with voice communication), share your screen (great for having people view a presentation from your PC), capture the current screen (it will capture the view of the current video participants), share a YouTube video with participants, share a document from Google Drive (better if done from personal Drive account), or remote desktop. The Remote desktop control is a great tool if you need access to update or repair something on another person's desktop PC. This actually allows you to remotely control their PC (with their permission).

Hangouts also allows you to add more apps to the environment that are Hangout compatible. This is a vast collection of apps available from the Recent apps (the ... on the menu). These tools add a lot of value and I urge you to experiment with them to find the best tools for you and your team to use.

Social Media Aspects: Pinterest

Most Social Media sites involve easy to see dialogue between parties. With an image-sharing site such as Pinterest, it's sometimes confusing to people that it is also Social Media. Pinterest is very similar to Facebook – albeit it is far more geared towards image sharing than the wealth of shares you find in Facebook or any other similar social media site.

Pinterest has gained a reputation of being a great (image-based) marketing tool. In fact, it's one of the top sources for web-based marketing and sales revenue. Photos of people using a particular product or a variety of product images lead people to click on the images for more information and will eventually make their way to the ecommerce website to make a purchase. From the aspect of causes or campaigns, using Pinterest presents a bit of a dilemma: What is the Product?

If you're working well on your mission and messaging, then you already know that you have a product. How you describe it for others determines how you can present it in an image-based platform such as Pinterest.

Consider a campaign for a candidate for public office. The "product" is the candidate. Photographs of the candidate shaking hands with the public, kissing babies, speaking at a forum, and the like are all useful photographs and images you can place within a Pinterest feed. Further, your candidate campaign or cause can be supported with images in the form of InfoGraphics, charts, memes and similar.

Pinterest will give you access to social media users who aren't either on Facebook or Twitter or any of the others or who aren't as active. Perhaps they use a portion of their brain that is more image-centered than text (like a Twitter user would have). In any case, you may decide to utilize Pinterest as part of your overall messaging by using Pinterest to not only host your images (like a Flickr account would do), but to drive engagement in the images as content.

If you've ever used a pinboard, then the concept behind Pinterest is an easy grasp. It's commonly used to post photos, graphics, recipes, and the like. People will use Pinterest to share their hobbies, favorite photos and interests with others via "pinning", "re-pinning" and liking. The concept of social image bookmarking is expanded with Pinterest. Facebook had already allowed for social image bookmarking. However, Pinterest concentrates on the images as the content for all posts. Pinterest users can upload, save, sort and manage images, photos, graphics and similar files (known as pins) within collections known as pinboards.

Different images can be grouped on different pinboards (similar to different albums within other sites). Users can browse other pinboards for images that interest them. This is made easier for most users by using a theme for each pinboard that will coincide with generalized themes from Pinterest (for example, movie buffs would post to "Film, Music & Books").

First, let's consider what Pinterest's basic functions are. Pinterest is a tool that allows users to share their visual content with others. This can be a sharing for projects, interests or similar. It's used extensively for sharing fun topics and ideas such as craft ideas, cooking and baking projects and DIY home projects. Beyond that, it has uses for Pop Culture photo sharing, fan art, and many other "image as content" projects. Each pin is a visual bookmark that can be shared with others. When a user clicks your pin, they can be transported back to your website. This is why it's important to have visually appealing pins for your campaign.

When you've figured out what bookmarks or Pins you want to have shared with others, you just need to figure out how to organize them. This can be the key.

You start out by creating a board (to which the pins are placed, just like a real bulletin board with pinned notes and photos). Give it a good name. Something obscure won't help you engage people.

Pinterest 1: Pin Board creation

As you create your board, you can enable the map feature so that similar location pins from other people help expose your pins. In the example above, local cities can be used on a Pin board in the category of Travel. While campaigning isn't interesting, Travel can be.

After you create a board, you can always edit it again or delete it. Be careful when deleting, once gone, it's gone.

Boards that you create are available for others to pin as well. All you do is invite others to pin using the "Who can add Pins?" field on the Edit Board screen. This is especially useful if you're working as a team on pinning.

You will start pinning using the board or boards you've created. The most effective way to drive traffic back to your website (which is one major goal in any campaign) is to first place good image-based content on your website. Then, you pin that content to the Pinterest board you created. There is a very useful shortcut to this if you have your HTML capable webmaster add the Pinterest code (Javascript) that turns your web site's photos and images into pinnable objects. (Visit developers.pinterest.com for information on how to do this.)

Let's say you have a photograph of a candidate for public office speaking to a large crowd. Having people in the image other than the candidate makes the photograph more compelling to people in the Pinterest world. Maybe they know someone in the photograph. Maybe they think they know someone and want to share it with others. An easy way to pin that photograph to Pinterest is to right click (with a PC) or ctrl-click (with a Mac) the image you want to pin and copy the URL for the image. Switch to Pinterest and click the "+" (the pin button). The menu gives you three choices. Whenever possible, stay away from using the "Upload a Pin" since it only loads the image content to Pinterest and doesn't directly link back to your web site. Use the "Add from a website" function whenever possible. Click this option.

Pinterest 2: Loading a Pin

Since you've already copied to your clipboard the link for the photograph, simply paste this link into the small URL field you see. This will capture the image you have at that location and display any pin-ready images on a selection screen. Find the photograph you would like to pin (using this method, there should be only one) and click the red "Pin it" button. Select the board for the pin and Pinterest will allow you to edit the description of the pin (the photograph).

Add a Pin from a website   ✕

Easily add Pins from any site with our handy Pin It button.

Pick a board

Pinterest 3: Adding a Pin from a sample URL

If you've already linked Facebook and Twitter to Pinterest (highly recommended), then check the selections for the respective social media sites. The description field is searchable and this is very important. In this description you can use hashtags. Since you should already be using some form of hashtags for your cause or mission, remember to use them within or at the end of your description text. Like metadata for YouTube descriptions, Pinterest descriptions for pins should contain key information that will allow searches to find the content and link back to the home base of your website.

It's a Secret

Secret Boards are available within Pinterest. Use these for sharing with your team and perhaps the 'special people' or fans of your campaign. This gives them a feeling of exclusivity. Think of it as an inner circle that is able to see your special posts. This is ideal for sharing progress on fundraising with donors or special events with volunteers and activists. People love to see their own photographs or group photos that contain their friends. Make these Secret Boards and load them with 'team' photos.

Let's have the Info (Graphics)

Infographics are becoming hugely popular. They are quite simple visuals that are used to represent data. Some people label these as Data Visualization tools. If you're familiar with the old expression "A picture is worth a thousand words" then an infographic helps you visualize a thousand (or lots more) points of data.

On a Pinterest post (or, Facebook or other graphic capable social media site), you can use an infographic to help underscore a position or message from your campaign or cause. Let's say you'd like to represent to your audience how many households have children in public schools. An infographic could have a stick drawing of a neighborhood to represent a city and simplified drawings of children in the houses to represent a 'Chart' of the total households that have students in the public schools. If 9 out of 10 houses show children, then the interpretation or "Visualization" of the data is that 90% of the households have children in public schools.

Infographics take many forms. They can be Venn diagrams, bar charts, a combination of images and data, Word Clouds, Polar graphs, pie graphs and so much more. One key to infographics is that they are the *shiny objects* of data. Face it; they catch people's attention. Even most poorly designed infographics will attract a glance from most users. Well-designed infographics are like fly traps – very sticky and engaging. This is why so many infographics are brightly colored and have easy to understand tidbits of data embedded within them. They aren't typically loaded down with numbers and text. The numbers and text provide a guide to the data but aren't really what holds people – it's the graphics representing the data. Because of this, infographics are shared far more than the average post to a blog, Tumblr or even Twitter.

Here are some tips for getting started on infographics:

- ✓ Keep each one simple. KISS principle works.

- ✓ Give the answer (text or text to help the audience come to a conclusion quickly)

- ✓ Cite your sources (footnoted information on the data's source lends credibility)

- ✓ Keep a pleasant color theme (don't make it too shocking)

- ✓ Send people home (If people are sharing your infographic, don't you want the recipients to know it came from you? Include your website information and/or social media names)

Some sites that help you generate infographics with ease:

- ✓ Infogr.am
- ✓ Piktochart.com
- ✓ Agbeat.com
- ✓ Charts.hohli.com
- ✓ Creately.com
- ✓ Google.com/publicdata

Social Media Aspects: Instagram

Pinterest is a visually rich environment. It allows for people to share photographs and other images with other from Desktops and mobile devices. Instagram, is geared more toward the Mobile user. For some, it's a combination of Pinterest (photo sharing with some descriptions) and Flickr (photo hosting mainly). The biggest reason that you really shouldn't ignore Instagram: It's used by a significant portion of Millennials and Teens.

Instagram is essentially an easy to use online sharing service for videos and photos. It integrates smoothly with social media sites (such as Facebook, Twitter and Tumblr) to allow for full social media sharing. Additionally, it has a series of special 'filters' for photographs that digitally enhance otherwise boring pictures. Many people will link their Instagram accounts with Flickr to store their 'finished' product in Flickr.

Instagram only allows for images to originate from a Mobile Phone (Digital Camera). This may limit some people, but it shouldn't stop you from using it in your campaign or cause. Find someone with a smartphone who can load Instagram's app and run with it.

Instagram is reliant on the social network. You should have friends and followers for Instagram to be effective for you. If you're using Instagram as an individual, you can use an Instagram account as an organization as well. Create an account with an email for the organization and share this information with others on the team who will be using Instagram for the cause. If you're taking photographs (or loading images from the camera's existing gallery or roll), you can apply a digital filter and share the photograph in Instagram's photo feed. If your friends and fellow activists are on Instagram (as individuals), you can further share the photos that show up in your stream. Getting people to follow your organization's Instagram account is similar to getting them to follow a Facebook or Twitter account: Load the stream with useful and interesting content and people will find it and share it. The more shares, the greater the opportunity for more people to follow your Instagram posts.

Getting followers in Instagram as an individual is fairly simple, especially since Facebook integrates directly. Your photos will post to your FB timeline as you send them from Instagram (you have to select this option as you post the photo). This can also be done on other platforms (such as Twitter). Sharing the photographs (and videos!) from Instagram through the other social media sites will lead people back to Instagram where, hopefully, they will follow you.

Get people in your personal networks to comment on photos posted in Instagram. This will increase the exposure on the social network for the photographs you post. This, in turn, will induce people to follow you. You may find people to follow in Instagram who interest you or have similar interests as you. From a cause or campaign perspective, this is a little more difficult since you're not as likely to find people displaying photographs of related items to your mission. But, you may find people with complementary items. These people may turn out to be "Like minded" and would be interested in viewing your posts. If you follow them, they will get a notification of the follow and may follow you. Reciprocity works well in Instagram since most of the people on the network tend to like to "show off" their photographs.

Adding a Twist

Instagram allows you to load any photograph or image from your camera roll (or gallery). Because of this, some people are able to take advantage and share images that are designed to communicate a message. Infographics, mentioned earlier, can be saved as jpg files on your smartphone and loaded into Instagram. The process for this varies slightly by platform.

Since Instagram isn't really about follower count, it's a good thing to know that you should take some liberty here. Post photographs of engaging, funny, unusual and other subjects. A dog wearing socks will get likes. Why? It's unusual and people react to it. If your feed includes photographs like this, the people who follow you will **still** be likely to see the photographs you post related to your cause or campaign.

Instagram has evolved into a community where people share moments in their lives. It's a good idea to share frequently in Instagram without expecting others to follow or comment on your photographs. If you're sharing the photos on your other social media platforms (choosing to share from the post on Facebook, Twitter and others is extremely handy to getting additional image-based content on all social networks) then you're using Instagram mostly as a distribution tool for your images – this is a great method. Instagram will allow you to build a following within its community while boosting your following and interest level outside (in other networks) of Instagram.

Lights, Camera, Action

Instagram now supports video uploads. Similar to the Vine service (from Twitter), Instagram uses a tap and hold feature to digitally record videos up to 15 seconds in length. You can hold the 'button' down for all 15 seconds to catch a length of action or use clever techniques to hold it for bursts and create a 'stop-action' video with special effects. Instagram video also includes some fun digital filters similar to what you will find in the photograph feature of Instagram. Videos, like Photographs, shared from Instagram, can be shared outside of the Instagram community to other social media platforms.

Things to Remember about Instagram

Instagram profiles are public (visible by all) by default. If you want to change this, you can create a private account. This means only the users you approve may follow you and see your images. This is changed in your profile tab (on your phone) under Privacy.

Instagram provides a feed of notifications for activities on your photos. Use this to see how much engagement you get on your posts. Enabling Push Notifications on your phone for Instagram may be a bit burdensome (you will get lots of notifications) if you post a lot of photos. Otherwise, you may want to use the push notifications for a little while to see what impact you have on the community.

Remember to tag other Instagram users to images, whenever possible. This will increase your exposure for the images.

Take the time to set up the social sharing settings in Instagram. You can see these in the Profile tab under Sharing Settings. You'll need to initially log in to the accounts you want to share to, but it's worth it. This way, all of your photos (as you elect) will automatically post to the other social media sites (such as Facebook, Twitter,

Flickr, Tumblr and Foursquare). This is something you can enable once and then choose photo by photo whether to share. This is a timesaver and will help you increase your reach.

Working with Photos

Taking a photo in Instagram is fairly easy and really doesn't require much explanation. Experiment with your first few photos. Post the ones you really like to your social media streams.

After you've gained some comfort with the basics, be sure to spend time using the various features of the Digital Filters, Borders and Tilt-Shift. The filters give you the controls needed to make otherwise boring photos pop. Tilt-Shift allows you to use selective focus with a custom depth of field to bring out certain parts of your image. Use this to emphasize key elements of a photo.

Sharing is Caring

Sharing from Instagram has been mentioned before. Getting a set of techniques in place that you can use frequently is important to maximize the effectiveness of your Instagram shares to other networks.

When you have a photo ready for sending and you are at the Share screen, take the time to tag any users (from Instagram) that are in the photo or who should benefit (tagging doesn't have to mean that the person is in the photo, it can mean you want that photo to show in their photo stream). Also, use the "@" to properly tag people in your description for people who are on Twitter. This is especially useful as you share your photos on your Twitter feed. Let's say you have a photograph of volunteers working on a project for a non-profit cause. Two of the people in the photograph have Instagram accounts, so you tag them from Instgram (using the tag people function). The non-profit has a Twitter account named @CleanNCParks so you tag it in the description (at the top of the screen next to the thumbnail of your final image) with the "@" as appropriate. You can then use the proper hashtags to bring attention to the post when it shows in the various social media sites that use hashtags (such as Twitter and Facebook). One last item you can activate that is very useful is the Photo Map. When you choose this, Instagram will help you locate the event or activity so you can tag the location. This will help categorize your image based upon location. This information will also be visible to others, so use it with discretion.

Here's an example of what the final post would look like before you post in Instagram:

Instagram 1: Rich post in Instagram

Other Social Media Sites

The social media sites covered with some detail in this guide are not the only social media tools available to the activist. However, they are the primary platforms and channels for the best "bang for the buck". Other sites have some usefulness in activism. This list will always be fluid as new sites are created while other sites are changed. Changes and innovations in the social media marketplace happen weekly.

I've included a brief list of additional Social Media sites that can contribute to a cause or campaign. If you have a resource or team-member available to spend time on one or more of these, then additional channels can and should be considered. Again, each channel should stress the message from your cause.

LinkedIn

Professionals gravitate to the social media site of LinkedIn. When it was created, LinkedIn targeted professionals to allow them to network for job prospects, projects and collaboration. LinkedIn allows people to build *connections* with contacts with which they have some relationship. LinkedIn requires some acknowledgement of a relationship before the connection can be created.

While a very powerful and significant social media tool, LinkedIn is not commonly used for activism. However, if you leverage your contacts within LinkedIn, it can prove to be a gold mine for grassroots supporters like yourself. LinkedIn also has tools that allow it to integrate with other social media platforms with shared postings.

Orkut

Orkut is a social media site managed under the Google umbrella of sites and services. It allows for building new connections, re-connecting with known associates and maintaining relationships – similar to Facebook. Orkut's largest user base is outside of the United States (in India and Brazil).

Tumblr

Tumblr (listed as tumblr for most) is an odd entry into the social media world. It's akin to a cross with Facebook and Twitter and Wordpress. While it's formally a short-form blogging site (contrasted to the micro-blog format of Twitter), it ties in similar aspects of the social networking (tags, for example) like Facebook. Tumblr was recently acquired by Yahoo and this purchase worries many in the tech industry. This is mainly because of Yahoo's track record with prior acquisitions.

Since Tumblr has a respected SEO footprint (availability of content to search engine results), it's a good idea to investigate and use Tumblr if you're already utilizing other social media platforms with success. For some, Tumblr is a better solution than using Wordpress for their "home" website. It's free (similar to the free site option of Wordpress) and it's really simple to get started on a Tumblr site. It's linkage to other social media sites is commendable, thus making a strong choice for any campaign.

Appendix

Common Twitter Hashtags

Hashtags give you a direction for the intent of the Twitter post. It's like a label for the reader to easily understand the agenda for the message. Additionally, it's a good way to identify a tweet with a group, a location, a day or similar. This way, it will show in the search results for anyone wishing to view that topic. For example, #Raleigh may be the location of your tweet's event. It will help people identify and relate to you more if they are in Raleigh and see the hashtag – even if the tweet is read after the event.

A side benefit, but completely worthy of mention is the hashtag gives you a topic to keep track of the conversation. If you watched any of the Presidential candidate debates in 2012 on TV, you may have seen the hashtags used by the media. For example, #CNNDebate may have been used to help others Tweet to a common conversation. If you and your group use the hashtags judiciously, you will have a way for people to jump in on your topic by using the same hashtag. If you do this frequently, you can use hashtags in your marketing materials. Then, set up a Twilert to keep track of the hashtag's progress and status (http://www.twilert.com/).

Checking trends in Hashtags can be useful too. The web site http://www.hashtags.org/analytics allows you to track trends in Twitter's hashtags.

Common Hashtags

#Happy

#FF (for Friday Follow: Used to share a list of Twitter accounts with the world)

#Fail

#Followback

#follow

#tlot (True Liberal on Twitter)

#tcot (True Conservative on Twitter)

#teaparty

#gop

#tpot

#StopCommonCore

#dwts

#glee

#app

#ipad

#android

#edtech

#socialgood

#change

#4change

#cause

#volunteer

Also, there are other Social Media tools (websites) that use hashtags:

Catch.com

Facebook

Fluidinfo

FriendFeed

Google+

Instagram

Orkut

Pinterest

Tumblr

Twitter

YouTube

All websites under Gawker Media

Diaspora software

Common Twitter Abbreviations

CC = Carbon-copy. Did you know this meant the same in email?

PRT = Partial retweet. The tweet you're looking at is the truncated version of someone else's tweet.

HT = Hat tip. This is a way of acknowledging a link to another Twitter user.

MT = Modified tweet. This means the tweet you're looking at is a paraphrase of a tweet originally written by someone else.

RT = Retweet (another user).

Common Shortcuts/Abbreviations for Texting, Tweets and more

ATM = At The Moment

B4 = Before

BBL = Be Back later

BFF = Best friend forever

BOL = Best of Luck

BRB = Be Right Back

BTW = By The Way

FWIW = For What it's Worth

FYI = For Your Information

GL = Good Luck

GR8 = Great

HF = Have Fun

HRU = How Are You?

IAC = In any Case

IC = I See

IDK = I Don't Know

IMHO = In my Humble Opinion

IMO = In My Opinion

IRL = In real Life

JK = Just Kidding

L8R = Later

LMAO = Laughing My Ass Off

LOL = Laughing Out Loud

LTNS = Long Time, No See

NM = Never Mind

NOYB = None of Your Business

NP = No Problem

OIC = Oh, I See

OMG = Oh My Goodness (or God)

OMW = On My Way

OTW = Off To Work

PLZ = Please

PPL = People

RL = Real Life

ROTFL= Rolling on the Floor Laughing

RTFM = Read the Fracking (or similar) Manual

SPST = Same Place, Same Time

TBD = To Be Determined

THX = Thanks

TTFN = Ta ta for Now

TTYL = Talk to You Later

WB = Welcome Back

WTF = What the F...?

WTG = Way to Go!

Plus you can find many more using Google or Bing or at the following site: http://textingabbreviationslist.com/

Tips for All Social Media

1. If someone is redistributing your content – Good! (Offer to help them out.)

2. Know the Return on Investment

3. Being Clever is better than Trying to be Clever.

4. Measure more than Followers.

5. Always try to "Link" your Tweets (include a hashtag or URL or @ reference).

6. Keep all social messaging personal whenever possible ("Joe the Activist" is regarded better than "Some faceless group"). This helps you connect on a personal level.

7. Leverage word of mouth with Paid Ads.

8. Long relationships are preferred over short (lean away from short term gifts).

9. Leverage GROUPS from social media, not just individuals.

10. If you don't update content, don't work with social media.

11. Use the appropriate HTML/Javascript code for any social media platform to embed the proper link to your Web page. For example, a "Like" button on your website that likes it on Facebook.

Chat Commands from Google Hangout

Available Commands from Google Hangouts Chat:

/to, /msg [user] [message] - Sends an inline private message to the specified user.

/shortcuts - Open keyboard shortcut help screen

/help, /? - Displays a list of command descriptions and usages.

/goto [user] - Opens the profile of the specified user in a new tab.

/mute - Mutes the audio of the caller.

/unmute - Unmutes the audio of the caller.

/vmute - Mutes the video of the caller.

/unvmute - Unmutes the video of the caller.

/topic [new topic] - Changes the title of the Hangout.

/users - Displays a list of users in the Hangout.

Useful Hangout Tip

To create a Hangout for your Community or group with a fixed (static) URL start by creating the Hangout from within Google Calendar. Schedule the event and add video call to the event. The link provided will be a permalink. Use this link in the Hangout invitations and other sharing methods with your team.

Advertising in Facebook

Facebook advertising is not free, but if used properly, can give you an effective way to reach more people with your marketing objective.

Advertising within campaigns and ad sets with the tools provided in Facebook allow for multiple demographic groups and more specific targeting for your ads. Further ads can be targeted smoothly within the desktop or mobile versions of Facebook.

Just like with your overall project campaign objective, you should determine what your Facebook advertising objective is. Let's consider the following scenarios:

1) My cause needs more people to see my Event.

2) My cause's Facebook Page needs more likes.

3) My cause's Facebook Page needs more visitors (engagement of page).

4) I need people to visit the Cause website after seeing my ad in Facebook.

With the objectives described in 1, 2, and 3 you will need to do some advanced homework. If you wish to advertise for an event or a page, then the page or event will need to exist in Facebook prior to creating the ad. If you're trying to drive people to your website (item 4), then you need to already have a website.

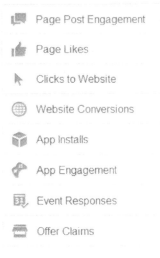

Page Post Engagement

Page Likes

Clicks to Website

Website Conversions

App Installs

App Engagement

Event Responses

Offer Claims

Facebook 4: Ad Objectives available

If you are going to advertise for your Facebook page, you must have permission (from the Page's settings) to create ads for the Page. (You will need to have the role of Admin, Editor, Moderator or Advertiser to have ad creation permission for your Page.)

Facebook advertising also supports other objectives such as downloading an App or file or directing people to a Facebook App.

After you have chosen your objective, gather your images for the ad. There are numerous schools of thought on ad image selection. I'll cover what I know works best for the campaigns I've used. These are:

1) Use quickly recognizable images without small text or detail.

2) Be sure the image is eye-catching in small and large formats (this is because the image will be displayed both ways).

3) Be sure the image is directly (or closely) related to your mission.

Choosing ad images for a cause or campaign is not as simple as choosing an image set for a product campaign. With a product, you can show consumers actually using the product. This gives the consumer a quick idea of the product's use. This can be as simple as an image drinking a cup of coffee from a coffee shop (where the coffee shop is placing an ad to drive customers to their location). When selecting images for a cause, you have to understand the psychology of the consumer and their relationship to the cause.

If you want to call people to action against something, showing an image of that something and an unhappy person will trigger the expected emotional response from the viewer. If you want to call people to action for something, images of a happy person should be used. Ad images do not have to be of people. They can be things as long as the things support your mission. Let's say you're creating an ad set that targets pro-gun users. The objective is to get people to go against a candidate who is anti-gun. The classic "anti" (the circle with a slash across it) symbolism can be used with a gun superimposed upon the image of the anti-gun politician can be used. This, at-a-glance, associates that candidate with the anti-gun stance.

Here's a list of proven ad image selection criteria:

- Happy woman looking directly at the camera

- Contrasting colors to Facebook (not blue and white) will make your image bounce

- Strong, easy to identify logos will "pop"

- Clear value proposition with graphics. For example, "Save 50% now" over an image of a person smiling and holding a piggy bank.

- InfoGraphics and solid value propositions (the

word "Free" works well) make the ad image more captivating. Be sure to not have small text

- If you have a video (or even if you don't) that you link the ad to, include a video "play" button on the bottom corner of the ad's image. It's a good idea to use video to support your ad.

- Children and pets (who can resist?) in images are often shared more than any other image type in Facebook

- Unusual images attract attention

- Human face with text overlay. This means use an open area of the photograph to insert easy to read text.

All in all, the number one image type is something that includes a human face. This just plain works.

When you've selected images, be sure to create some basic text that will go along with these images. You will have 90 characters to draw people to click on your ad's action button or the ad itself. The final ad is displayed with the 90 characters (max) and a total display of 100px by 72px (for a sidebar ad).

For all ads, the best image size to use is 1200x627 pixels. If you don't use this size, at least make sure the images you use are 600 pixels wide if you want the ad to appear in the news feed.

Use the combination of the image(s) you select and the text you use with the images in a test. It's ok and desirable to ask others what they think of the combination. Ask more than one person if you can. Once you've posted images and text with your ad (you'll do this step soon), you can gauge how the combination works (the ad effectiveness) with the tools available in your Ad Manager.

Your ad's demographics are valuable aspects to set. If you don't choose your settings wisely, you could end up having your ad displayed in areas (not just geographic, but demographic) that are just wasteful. Let's say you're trying to compel Seniors to take action. Your demographic settings include age group. If you neglect this, your ad will be displayed to other groups (not just Seniors) and the cost per impression will be higher than you should have.

In the following image, you will see that the selections for a fictional cause have been chosen to target Millennials living near Durham (within 25 miles) who are either in college now or have a college degree who rent (not own) and lean conservatively with some activism (donating is a form of activism). In addition, if you look at the Audience Definition on the right, you will see that they are not connected currently with the 4th District GOP (an existing Page in Facebook).

Facebook 5: Setting Ad Audience or Demographics

When you have determined the best (this is subjective and will change) demographics or audience to capture, you will name your ad set (and campaign, if you do not wish to keep the suggested name) and set your budget and schedule. Your budget, initially, should be relatively low (under $20 is often best) since you are going to be testing your ad effectiveness for the first range of time. If you set a high ad budget (per day) and your ad is improperly constructed or just plain ineffective, you will blow through your budget and not achieve any measurable results.

As you review this ad setting, note that you can schedule the ad to begin at a particular date in the future. This is especially handy if you have some tested ad copy that you'd like to deploy in ad sets (with images) at a certain time in your campaign or cause schedule. It's like a set and forget ad (but please don't forget to follow the metrics of the ad!).

CAMPAIGN AND AD SET

Campaign	Fourth District NC GOP - Page Likes Change Campaign
Ad Set Name	Durham - 18-35
Budget	Per day ▾ $50.00 USD
Schedule	• Run my ad set continuously starting today
	◦ Set a start and end date

Facebook 6: Budget and Ad Set info for Facebook ads

The last major setting is the bidding and pricing. This lets you optimize your campaign's ad objective. Some objectives may be to maximize clicks while others may be to maximize impressions (times the ad is visible to users of Facebook). Note that these two aren't really mutually exclusive. Determine if impressions or likes is part of your mission and make the better choice. Your choice may affect the Pricing selection. If it does, you typically are safe choosing the "Automatically optimize" pricing. If you'd like to manually set your maximum bid amount, you can still do that.

Once you finalize your ad, you will "Review Order". This will give you an Ad Name (change this to better describe the ad you are placing) along with the Audience and other settings for your ad set. Review the summary screen carefully before you click "Place Order". If you need to make changes (people often see mistakes made in the audience selection at this point), simply click "Edit Order" and make the necessary changes. Place the order when completed.

The ad will be reviewed at Facebook before going live. When the ad is live (remember, if you scheduled it for a later date, it will be reviewed first then posted on the scheduled date) you will see the metrics showing in your Ad manager. These will help you determine the effectiveness of your ad.

Also, if you chose more than one image in your ad creation, Facebook ad manager will have created an Ad Set with multiple ads with the same text – just different images. This is an extremely useful tool to help determine what images rank higher in user engagement.

In case you didn't already know, there are some terms which are very useful to understand before you delve into the features of an ad campaign (not just Facebook but Google Ads and other ads hosted elsewhere on the web).

- **CPC: Cost Per Click.** This is how much you will pay for the advertising per click from a visitor to the website for that particular ad.

- **CTR: Click Through Rate**. This is the percentage rate at which people click on the ad. Simply expressed as a percentage of the viewed versus the clicked. (Number of Clicks/Number of Impressions) X 100.

- **CPM: Cost Per Mille**. This is the cost per 1,000 impressions.

For ads that are political in nature, you will often find that increasing the CTR is more useful and beneficial than decreasing the CPC. Consider this as getting more people to "See" (impressions) your message rather than "Doing" (clicking on the ad). A higher CTR does mean more people are clicking "through" to your target URL (hopefully, your website). But, this also means that more people will be seeing your ad, even though they are not clicking if you have a low CTR (more views than clicks).

YouTube Metadata

When you add videos to YouTube, use the Title, Description and Tag fields of each video similar to what you may have used for the Channel set-up. Each Title should clearly bring people to understand what the video is about OR it should easily attract viewers to the video. The Description and Tags should be populated for ease of search and comprehension. If you think about it this way, it will make more sense: Description and Tags are used for Search Engines. The Tag is for Keywords. The Description is for key phrases. The Description will also appear alongside the video to help viewers decide whether to watch the video. Also, the Description will lead viewers to *more information* after they have watched the video (include the URL for your web site!).

Useful Twitter and other Social Media Tools

This is a partial list (new tools are created weekly, it seems) of very handy tools. Those in bold are highly recommended.

TweetDeck	**TweetDeck.com**
HootSuite	**HootSuite.com**
SproutSocial	sproutSocial.com
Crowdbooster	**crowdbooster.com**
SocialFlow	SocialFlow.com
Bit.ly	**Bit.ly**
Everypost	Everypost.me
Buffer	**Bufferapp.com**
Spredfast	**spredfast.com**
Tweepi	**Tweepi.com**
SocialOomph	socialoomph.com

Tools useful with social media

Eventbrite	**Eventbrite.com**
Apture	Apture.com
Skitch	Skitch.com
Flickr	**Flickr.com**
Authority Labs	**Authoritylabs.com**
TubeMogul	**tubemogul.com**
Google Alerts	**Google.com/alerts**
Blogger	**Blogger.com**
WordPress	**Wordpress.com**
StumbleUpon	**Stumbleupon.com**
Reddit	**reddit.com**

Vanity URLs

Setting a custom web address for your social media page or presence is a good idea. For example, if your cause is called "NC Better Schools" and you have set up a page called that, you can set your Facebook Web Address from the "Update Page Info" menu.

Facebook

Facebook will allow you to set the URL so it's easier to communicate to people. This makes it easier to have friends and potential supporters find you. For example, the web address Facebook.com/NCBetterSchools is better than facebook.com/pages/NCBetterSchools/282736634 any day!

Twitter

Twitter will automatically set your URL based upon the name of your Twitter handle. For example, if you are @NCBetterSchools then your Twitter URL would be Twitter.com/NCBetterSchools

Pinterest

When you set up your cause (as a business) in Pinterest, you can change your "Business Account Basics" to include the username (which becomes your URL). Under the Profile settings, you will see a place to change your business image (picture) and Username, among others.

Profile

Business Name	A Zombie Life
Picture	[mug image] Change Picture
Username	www.pinterest.com/ azombielife
About You	A Zombie Life is the home of the Zombie Paradise. You've heard of the Zombie Apocalypse, the Zombie Invasion... Now, it's time for a Zombie Life.
Location	
Website	http://www.azombielife.com/ ⊘ Site verified

When you make these changes, you will have a URL for your Pinterest similar to the structure Pinterest.com/NCBetterSchools.

Instagram

Instagram, like Twitter, gives you a really nice URL based upon your account's username. In this example you'd have Instagram.com/NCBetterSchools as your vanity URL.

Instagram, although mainly designed to originate

content from the mobile devices, works really well on the web from a desktop computer or laptop. Give people your Instagram URL for them to like your posts and more.

Google+

Google is a bit of the oddball when it comes to custom URL for your organization. First, you have to have been using the Google+ page for your organization for some time before they let you make any URL change. This is pretty easy though. All you need to do is post photos and content frequently to the Google+ page. You don't even have to do it daily. Just do it and don't ignore it.

After a while, Google will contact you (with a message at the top of your Profile page in Google+) and offer you a choice of URLs. It's important to start out your Google+ Page with a good name, because Google will take this name as your starting point for your vanity URL. Unfortunately, it doesn't always give you flexibility in its options from this name. So it's a good idea to get as close to the URL you desire the first time.

When you have been offered to select your URL name and have chosen one from the offered list, be sure to tell people the URL in the following format:

Google.com/+NCBetterSchools

You will note the + in the URL. This automatically will redirect in Google to plus.google.com/+NCBetterSchools. Since you don't want to have to tell people the long name, stick with the short one.

How to Leverage your URL

If you're using customized business cards for your cause or campaign, be sure to place the most used social media URLs on them. Don't just list name, title, organization, address and phone info. Go ahead and add the website for your cause and below (or above) consider placing a Facebook (F) logo with the URL next to it like:

When you tweet, post to FB or Google+ or any other platform, share other platforms' URLs to speed the engagement network. For example, when posting in Twitter and you have room to spare, remind people of your Facebook page by including the URL: http://www.facebook.com/NCBetterSchools

If you do any posters or banners for public events, be sure to generate graphics like the FB example above with your various URLs. You can use simply an Icon image for each Social Media platform with the URL specific to you. When people see the banner and react to it, they may just take out their mobile phone and engage with you right then and there.

A Bit about Bit.ly

Using a URL shortener is a good idea with many posts. Twitter, Facebook and other platforms will automatically shorten your URLs for you when you make a post. However, it's not so easy to *track* your posts this way. If you use Bit.ly, your URLs are shortened and they are tracked. You simply have to create a Bit.ly account and use it to shorten your URLs.

Here's an example URL for an article:

http://saynotocommoncore.net/national-opt-out-refuse-the-test-campaign/

Here's the same example shortened with bit.ly:

http://bit.ly/1kqwcll

The shortening feature is the reason you use Bit.ly, the analytics is why you stick with Bit.ly. Analytics on each of the links you've created. You will discover where they are shared (such as Facebook and Twitter) and how many clicks were on the links. It's a wealth of information for any person trying to gauge their content sharing engagement.

Take a look at the sample metrics from Bit.ly on the next page and you will see a small example of the great metrics. One link (in the example) was shared 5 times over the course of one 24 hr period. Three hits on Facebook and two on Twitter. You can see the times the clicks occurred. Other data includes "where" in the world it traveled.

Clicks

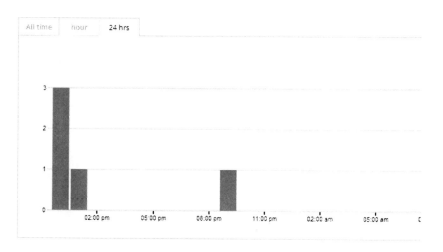

Where This Bitlink Was Shared

The Basics 2: Bit.ly graph on a shortened link